The Dangers of
Marijuana

Carla Mooney

ReferencePoint
Press®

San Diego, CA

About the Author

Carla Mooney is the author of many books for young adults and children. She lives in Pittsburgh, Pennsylvania, with her husband and three children.

© 2017 ReferencePoint Press, Inc.
Printed in the United States

For more information, contact:
ReferencePoint Press, Inc.
PO Box 27779
San Diego, CA 92198
www.ReferencePointPress.com

LIBRARY OF CONGRESS CATALOGING-IN-PUBLICATION DATA

Names: Mooney, Carla, 1970- author.
Title: The dangers of marijuana / by Carla Mooney.
Description: San Diego, CA : ReferencePoint Press, Inc., 2017. | Series: Drug dangers | Includes bibliographical references and index.
Identifiers: LCCN 2015048435 (print) | LCCN 2016005208 (ebook) | ISBN 9781682820209 (hardback) | ISBN 9781682820216 (epub)
Subjects: LCSH: Marijuana--Juvenile literature. | Marijuana abuse--Juvenile literature.
Classification: LCC HV5822.M3 M66 2017 (print) | LCC HV5822.M3 (ebook) | DDC 362.29/5--dc23
LC record available at http://lccn.loc.gov/2015048435

CONTENTS

CHAPTER 1: The Scope of Marijuana Use

For students at South Glens Falls Senior High School in New York, smoking marijuana is fairly common. Students smoke marijuana on school property, at sporting events, and even behind the elementary school building before or after school hours. Some students have posted videos on social media of themselves smoking marijuana while standing in the lunch line. "I know people who have snuck it to school. I know people who are using it for stress-relievers,"[1] says Teyler Nassivera, a senior at the high school. To avoid getting caught, Nassivera says that students put marijuana into e-cigarettes, battery-operated devices that deliver the drug in vapor form instead of smoke, which reduces marijuana's telltale smell.

Wanting to understand the extent of student marijuana use, in 2014 the South Glens Falls Central School District conducted a survey of approximately 1,150 students in grades seven through twelve. In the survey, one in four high school juniors and seniors admitted to smoking marijuana within the past thirty days. Jenn Wood, a coordinator for the Community Coalition for Family Wellness, a group that works to reduce youth substance abuse, says that school officials are concerned about the large numbers of teens using marijuana. Especially concerning is the number of eighth graders who admitted to smoking marijuana, which rose from 5 percent in 2011 to 8 percent in 2014. South Glens Falls school officials are concerned that using marijuana at such a young age puts teens at risk for future health problems and opens the door to additional drug use. "Those who end up using cocaine or heroin have a much greater chance of having start[ed] with something like alcohol, marijuana or tobacco,"[2] says Wood.

Officials at South Glens Falls are not alone in their concerns. Across the country, marijuana use is increasing. According to a 2015 report published in *JAMA Psychiatry*, nearly 10 percent of adults inhaled or ingested marijuana in 2013, as compared to 4 percent in 2001. Although many users will experience no long-term effects, others may become addicted or suffer permanent damage.

What Is Marijuana?

Marijuana is a drug that comes from the dried leaves, flowers, stems, and seeds of the hemp plant, known as *Cannabis sativa*. It has many street names, including pot, weed, herb, grass, bud, ganja, and Mary Jane. The cannabis plant contains more than five hundred chemicals, about one hundred of which are compounds called cannabinoids. One of these cannabinoids, delta-9-tetrahydrocannabinol (THC), is a mind-altering chemical that produces the psychoactive effect experienced by marijuana users. THC is found in the resin produced by the leaves and buds of the cannabis plant.

Users say that marijuana makes them feel relaxed and mellow and gives them a sense of haziness. Some users report having increased sensory perception, such as being able to see brighter colors. Others report an altered perception of time and increased appetite. Jared, who lives in Washington, DC, where marijuana use is legal, says that he often smokes at night after his children have gone to bed. "It relaxes me. And it helps me get perspective to see the big picture. I find that enjoyable,"[3] he says. Sometimes, using marijuana is less pleasant. Some users report that initial feelings of relaxation and euphoria can later turn to paranoia and panic.

> "Those who end up using cocaine or heroin have a much greater chance of having start[ed] with something like alcohol, marijuana or tobacco."[2]
>
> —Jenn Wood, a coordinator for Community Coalition for Family Wellness, a group that works to reduce youth substance abuse.

Who Uses Marijuana?

Marijuana is the most commonly used illicit drug in the United States. According to a 2015 Gallup Poll, 44 percent of Americans admitted they have tried it at some point during their lives, and millions currently use it. According to the Substance Abuse and Mental Health Services Administration's (SAMHSA) 2014 National Survey on Drug Use and Health, 22.2 million people aged twelve and older reported using marijuana in the past month. Some of the heaviest users are adults aged eighteen to twenty-five, with nearly 20 percent of this age group reporting they had used the drug in the past thirty days.

In fact, age is one of the most significant factors related to marijuana use. According to the 2015 Gallup Poll, whether a person has used or currently uses marijuana significantly varies by age. Whereas adults aged thirty to sixty-four are most likely to admit to trying marijuana, Americans younger than thirty are more likely to say that they currently use it (18 percent). Those in the oldest age group surveyed—sixty-five and older—were the least likely to say they currently use marijuana (3 percent) or have ever tried it (22 percent). Across age groups, gender is also a factor, with men being more than twice as likely as women to use marijuana—13 percent compared to 6 percent.

Marijuana use is also widespread among teens, with older teens being more likely to use it than younger ones. According to the National Institute on Drug Abuse's (NIDA) 2014 Monitoring the Future survey, 21.2 percent of twelfth graders reported that they had used the drug within the past thirty days, compared to 16.6 percent of tenth graders and 6.5 percent of eighth graders. For seniors, marijuana was their drug of choice, even more popular than cigarettes (13.6 percent). In fact, nearly 6 percent of twelfth graders said that they used marijuana every day.

Smoking and Vaping

Typically, users hand roll marijuana leaves into cigarettes (called joints) and smoke them. Alternatively, users can smoke marijuana in small pipes or water pipes called bongs. Others smoke mari-

In recent years, several states have legalized marijuana for medical and recreational use. These changes may have led to the rising belief among teens that marijuana is harmless. As more teens believe smoking pot is a low-risk activity, more are experimenting with the drug.

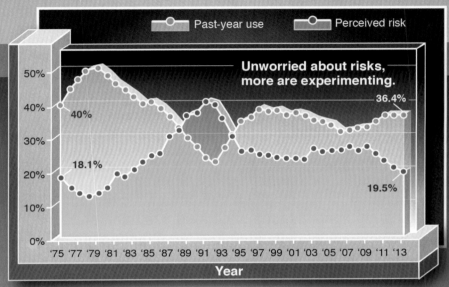

High school seniors' past-year marijuana use and the perceived risk of using the drug

Source: Liz Szabo, "Marijuana Poses More Risks than Many Realize," *USA Today*, July 30, 2014. www.usatoday.com.

juana in what are known as blunts, which are emptied cigar wrappers that have been refilled with marijuana.

In recent years, another way to use marijuana has emerged—vaping, which involves using e-cigarette devices, called vaporizers or vape pens. A vaporizer heats regular plant marijuana to a temperature lower than that needed to burn. The user draws air through the heated marijuana, which causes it to emit a vapor that contains THC. Because the marijuana never burns when vaping, there is no smoke. Marijuana concentrates such as hash oil are also used in vaporizers.

Vaping is increasingly popular with teens. In a 2015 survey of nearly four thousand high school students conducted by researchers at Yale University, 28 percent said they had tried e-cigarettes, and nearly one in five of those said they had also tried to vape marijuana. One reason vaping is becoming more common is because it allows users to be more discreet with their drug use. "It's so much easier to conceal e-cigarette pot use," says Meghan Rabbitt Morean, an assistant professor at Oberlin College. "Everyone knows that characteristic smell of marijuana, but this vapor is different. It's possible that teenagers are using pot in a much less detectable way."[4] Nikki Esquibel, a nineteen-year-old from California who has a prescription for medical marijuana, says that she uses a vaporizer pen. It is sleek and black. "I use it mostly around my neighborhood," says Esquibel. "It's easy to hide,"[5] in part because the vapor emitted from the device does not have much of an odor.

> "Everyone knows that characteristic smell of marijuana, but this vapor is different. It's possible that teenagers are using pot in a much less detectable way."[4]
>
> —Meghan Rabbitt Morean, an assistant professor at Oberlin College.

Many people use marijuana concentrates, resins that have been chemically extracted from the plant, in vape pens. Whereas marijuana flowers contain up to about 20 percent THC, concentrates can be much stronger, containing up to 90 percent THC. Vaping marijuana concentrates can therefore have much stronger effects than anticipated. Esquibel says that she noticed the increased strength of the drug when she took her first hit from a vaporizer pen and almost fainted. Allen St. Pierre, executive director of the National Organization to Reform Marijuana Laws, a nonprofit group working to legalize marijuana use, says that increased THC levels associated with vaporizer pens is a concern. Most states that allow the sale and use of medical marijuana, such as California, do not have rules for marijuana concentrates or vaporizing pens. "This is a screaming call for regulation if there ever was one."[6]

Marijuana comes from the dried leaves, flowers, stems, and seeds of the hemp plant (pictured), known as Cannabis sativa. The plant contains more than five hundred chemicals, including THC, which produces a psychoactive effect in marijuana users.

Edible Marijuana

Marijuana edibles are food and drink products laced with the cannabis plant. Marijuana-laced brownies, cookies, root beer, tea, and other edible products are growing in popularity, particularly in communities where medical and recreational marijuana have been legalized. In Colorado, which legalized medical marijuana in 2000 and recreational marijuana in 2012, consumers purchased 5.8 million edible marijuana and concentrate products such as lollipops, cookies, and cakes in 2014, according to the Colorado Department of Revenue Annual Update. "Edibles are a very tantalizing, tempting way for people to experiment because they come in every form you can think of,"[7] says Jim Gerhardt, a longtime police officer and vice president of the Colorado Drug Investigators Association.

Because it is ingested instead of smoked, edible marijuana has a delayed effect on users as it passes through a person's digestive tract into the bloodstream. Typically, it takes at least one to two hours for a user to experience a marijuana high from an

Synthetic Marijuana

Synthetic marijuana is a designer, human-made drug that is created by spraying liquid chemicals on dried herbs or other shredded plant material to mimic the effect of THC, the main psychoactive ingredient in the marijuana plant. On the street, synthetic marijuana has several names, including Spice and K2. Frequently marketed as incense and labeled "not for human consumption," it has become a popular drug with high school students and young adults because it is easily purchased, is inexpensive, and does not show up on standard drug tests.

Many users believe that synthetic marijuana is safe to use and that it produces a similar effect to plant-based marijuana. However, the chemicals in this drug can be much stronger than the THC found in the cannabis plant. As a result, the effects of synthetic marijuana are often stronger and more unpredictable. In addition, users often do not know what chemicals are actually in what they buy, so adverse effects are unpredictable and can vary widely. Common side effects include agitation, rapid heartbeat, lethargy, nausea, vomiting, confusion, headaches, and seizures. Users have also reported psychotic effects such as extreme anxiety, paranoia, and hallucinations. In New York City there were more than twenty-three hundred emergency room visits related to synthetic marijuana in July and August 2015. "This is a very risky substance that carries significant health consequences," says Dr. Hillary Kunins, an assistant commissioner at the New York City Department of Health. "This is not a drug to be used lightly and . . . the effects are unpredictable and serious."

Quoted in Ashley Welch, "Why New York City Is Banning Synthetic Marijuana K2," CBS News, October 20, 2015. www.cbsnews.com.

edible product, as compared to smoking the drug (the effects of which are immediate). This delayed effect can be dangerous if users think the drug is not working and thus consume more than one serving. Consuming multiple servings of edible marijuana products at a time can lead to sedation, anxiety, psychosis, and other serious psychological effects.

In 2014 nineteen-year-old Levy Thamba Pongi, an exchange student from the Republic of the Congo who was visiting Colorado, died after eating a marijuana cookie. Pongi first ate one serving of the cookie, which was estimated to have 10 milligrams of THC. After not feeling any effects within thirty to sixty minutes, Pongi ate the rest of the cookie, which contained 65 milligrams of THC and constituted 6.5 servings in total (according to the label). Within a few hours Thamba began behaving violently. At one point he smashed room furniture, lamps, and a television. He ran from his hotel room and jumped over the balcony, falling four stories to his death. According to a report from the Centers for Disease Control and Prevention, Pongi's death "illustrates a potential danger associated with recreational edible marijuana use."[8] The report also cautioned that "because of the delayed effects of THC-infused edibles, multiple servings might be consumed in close succession before experiencing the 'high' from the initial serving, as reportedly occurred in this case. Consuming a large dose of THC can result in a higher THC concentration, greater intoxication, and an increased risk for adverse psychological effects."[9]

> "Edibles are a very tantalizing, tempting way for people to experiment because they come in every form you can think of."[7]
>
> —Jim Gerhardt, a longtime police officer and vice president of the Colorado Drug Investigators Association.

Marijuana Extracts

Another form of marijuana gaining popularity is extracts, also known as dabs. Extracts are the resins from the cannabis plant. Extracts range from a gooey liquid to a soft, solid, waxy substance that looks like either honey or butter. This appearance gives extracts common nicknames such as honey oil, budder, wax, and shatter. Typically, users smoke extracts using water or oil pipes in a process called dabbing. In recent years users are also using vaporizer pens to vape marijuana extracts.

Marijuana extracts are extremely high in THC. According to the Drug Enforcement Administration, the THC in extracts can range from 40 percent to 80 percent, as compared to 20 percent in high-grade marijuana. Because the THC in extracts is so highly concentrated, it produces a more intense physical and psychological high than smoking plant marijuana. "Dabs are four times

Marijuana candy and cookies are for sale in a coffee shop in the Netherlands. Marijuana-laced brownies, cookies, tea, and other edible products are growing in popularity, particularly in communities where medical and recreational marijuana have been legalized.

as strong as a joint, and the high is administered all at once,"[10] says John Stogner, assistant professor of criminology at the University of North Carolina–Charlotte. According to one young adult who has smoked marijuana extracts, "It's much more intense. It's like you go blank and you can't really comprehend the world around you. When it comes to dabs, it's a lot harder to focus on everyday tasks, your mind is there but it's not at the same time."[11]

It is not just consuming marijuana extracts that can be dangerous—the process of making them can be, as well. Ground marijuana leaves are cooked in a cylinder soaked with butane, a fuel commonly used in cigarette lighters. The mixture is heated to evaporate the butane, leaving the thick extract behind. The butane evaporates into the air as a highly flammable gas, and one small spark can trigger an explosion. "There's a big danger of fire even if they aren't using some sort of heating device," says Stogner. "Given the amount of butane that can build up during this process, these individuals should be worried about any spark from any source."[12] These explosions can have tragic results, causing property damage, injury, and even death. In December 2014 eighty-five-year-old Sally Douglas died from severe carbon monoxide poisoning and smoke inhalation after her grandson and his friend triggered a fire in her basement while attempting to make marijuana wax.

Debate over Legalization

Although marijuana use remains illegal for any reason under federal law, as of early 2016 twenty-three states and the District of Columbia had legalized its use to treat certain diseases and illnesses. Two main chemicals from the cannabis plant, THC and cannabidiol (CBD), have shown promise in medical use. THC has been shown to increase appetite, reduce nausea, decrease pain and inflammation, and assist with muscle control problems. CBD is also useful in reducing pain and inflammation and has been used to control seizures and for the treatment of mental illness and addiction. Illinois resident Bill Wilson believes that medical marijuana will help him manage the pain and inflammation caused by degenerative spinal disease and reduce his use of anti-inflammatory drugs and prescription painkillers. "This is going to be a godsend," he said upon making his first purchase of medical marijuana after Illinois opened its dispensaries in November 2015. "I really believe that."[13]

In addition, four states—Alaska, Colorado, Oregon, and Washington—and the District of Columbia have passed laws making it legal for adults to use marijuana recreationally, or for enjoyment. Additional states, including California, are considering legalizing recreational marijuana use. In many cases these states have already reduced penalties for people caught possessing marijuana. This may mean that the state will not prosecute or jail people caught with small amounts of marijuana for personal use.

In other states, like Nevada, people caught with a small amount of marijuana will no longer be jailed but can still be arrested and charged with a misdemeanor and face a heavy fine.

According to Morgan Fox, communications manager at the Marijuana Policy Project, having public support for marijuana legalization is critical to getting bills and referendums on a state's agenda. In many of the states that may soon legalize recreational marijuana, recent polls show a majority of people support legalization in some form. For example, in Connecticut 63 percent of respondents in a March 2015 Quinnipiac University poll said they favor legalizing the possession of small amounts of marijuana for adults.

The legalization of marijuana for medical and recreational uses may be influencing teen attitudes toward the drug and its risks. In a nationwide survey of drug use among teens, there has been a steep decline in the number who believe that marijuana use is risky. Since 1996, when California became the first state to legalize medical marijuana, the number of twelfth graders who believe

Public Opinion on Legal Marijuana

The majority of the American public supports legalizing marijuana. According to a Gallup Poll released in October 2015, 58 percent of adults thought marijuana should be legal—a number that had increased from 51 percent a year prior. Many legalization supporters say concerns over marijuana's safety are exaggerated, and the majority of people who use the drug do so responsibly. They point out that marijuana is safer than many other legal drugs such as tobacco and alcohol, which are connected with a much higher risk of death from use and overdose. "There's more use overall because people are recognizing that marijuana use is not as harmful as they were led to believe," says Mason Tvert of the pro-legalization Marijuana Policy Project. Despite growing acceptance of marijuana, 40 percent of Gallup Poll respondents still believe that marijuana should remain illegal.

Quoted in Trevor Hughes, "Poll Says Marijuana Legalization Support Nears 60%," *USA Today*, October 21, 2015. www.usatoday.com.

that regular marijuana use is harmful has steadily dropped, from 59.9 percent in 1996 to 36.1 percent in 2014. These "results regarding marijuana are disappointing," says Gil Kerlikowske, director of the Office of National Drug Control Policy. "Making matters worse, more teens are now smoking marijuana than smoke cigarettes."[14]

Underestimating Marijuana

Many people believe that marijuana is not a dangerous drug and that it is safer and less addictive than alcohol or other illicit drugs. Experts warn, however, that this attitude may lead people to underestimate its dangers. "The potency of marijuana has skyrocketed, and along with that has come a new batch of mental health problems, emergency room mentions [that is, being the cause of an emergency room visit], learning deficiencies and school problems, and car crashes not seen in previous generations,"[15] says Kevin Sabet, president of Smart Approaches to Marijuana, an alliance of organizations and individuals dedicated to a health-first approach to marijuana policy. With this in mind, teens need to educate themselves about marijuana, its effects, and its risks before they decide to try it.

> "More teens are now smoking marijuana than smoke cigarettes."[14]
>
> —Gil Kerlikowske, director of the Office of National Drug Control Policy.

CHAPTER 2: Effects of Marijuana Use

How marijuana affects a person depends on a variety of factors, such as the type used, a person's size, and his or her history with the drug. A person with a faster metabolism will absorb the drug faster into his or her system, speeding up the effects. A person with a slower metabolism may experience the drug's effects more slowly.

The way a person uses marijuana can also influence its effects. When smoked or vaporized, marijuana's effects are usually felt within a few seconds of being inhaled and then quickly reach a peak that lasts from fifteen to thirty minutes. The drug's effects slowly decline and wear off over a few hours. If ingested in an edible form, the drug's effects may take longer to be felt—anywhere from thirty minutes to an hour. Once they emerge, the effects from edible marijuana are often abrupt and powerful and last about four to six hours.

Intensified Experiences

Marijuana intensifies everyday sensations and experiences. Some users say that while high, they are better able to focus and concentrate. Others like the fuzzy haze that marijuana casts over their environment. Either way, their moods, sensations, and experiences are all more intense. A user may feel as if he or she is hearing the best music ever listened to or eating the most delicious dessert in the world.

Many people who use marijuana report pleasant feelings of euphoria and relaxation. Anxiety may fade away as users begin to feel detached from their worries and the world around them. Perception of time and space may become altered, and some people may get the giggles or become extremely talkative. As one user describes the experience, "When I was high, I experienced a pervasive sense of calm and clarity. I felt effusive, funny, outgoing, and at ease in a way I had never known before."[16] For many these social feelings of enjoyment and relaxation are followed by drowsiness and sedation.

Other users believe that marijuana helps them tap into their creative side. For example, musician Graham Nash of Crosby, Stills & Nash explains in his 2013 autobiography, *Wild Tales: A Rock and Roll Life*, that he would write songs while high on marijuana. "Weed unlocked my mind and my emotions, which had to be awakened for me to start writing meaningfully," he claims. "It put [me] in a rapturous mood."[17]

The Dark Side of Marijuana

In other people, however, marijuana can bring on feelings of fear, anxiety, distrust, panic, mania, and paranoia. "Marijuana can cause panic attacks and a racing heartbeat—sometimes people are afraid they're having a heart attack,"[18] explains David Sack, CEO of Promises Treatment Centers, a provider of residential drug and alcohol rehabilitation. This was the experience of seventeen-year-old Lea from New Hampshire, who says, "I tried pot one time at a party, and I started to feel anxious and paranoid. My heart literally felt like it was about to explode; it was beating way too fast."[19] Marijuana can also temporarily impair people's ability to make decisions or judgments, making it more likely that they may engage in high-risk behaviors such as unprotected sex or driving while impaired.

> "Marijuana can cause panic attacks and a racing heartbeat—sometimes people are afraid they're having a heart attack."[18]
>
> —David Sack, CEO of Promises Treatment Centers.

If the concentration of THC is high or if users take large doses, they may experience acute psychosis, including hallucinations and delusions, and may lose their sense of identity. Other times, marijuana impairs short-term memory. A user may lose track of what he or she was saying a minute earlier or have a hard time learning and retaining new information.

New York Times columnist Maureen Dowd wrote about her scary experience with marijuana in 2014. While researching an assignment about marijuana legalization, the journalist ate a pot-laced candy bar that she purchased legally from a store in Denver, Colorado. At first Dowd felt little effect from the marijuana candy. About an hour after ingesting the drug, she began to experience severe anxiety and paranoia. "I felt a scary shudder go through my body and brain," she wrote in an article about the experience.

> I barely made it from the desk to the bed, where I lay curled up in a hallucinatory state for the next eight hours. I was thirsty but couldn't move to get water. Or even turn off the lights. I was panting and paranoid, sure that when the room-service waiter knocked and I didn't answer, he'd call the police and have me arrested for being unable to handle my candy. I strained to remember where I was or even what I was wearing, touching my green corduroy jeans and staring at the exposed-brick wall. As my paranoia deepened, I became convinced that I had died and no one was telling me.[20]

Overnight, the marijuana's effect slowly wore off, leaving Dowd shaken and confused. The next day she discovered that she had eaten more than the recommended dose of the candy bar, which probably explained her negative reaction.

Physical Effects

Within a few minutes after smoking marijuana, a person's heart rate increases. Whereas a normal heart rate falls between seventy and eighty beats per minute, marijuana can cause it to increase by twenty to fifty beats per minute or more. In some cases it can raise blood pressure and reduce the blood's oxygen-carrying capacity. According to the NIDA, there is some evidence that a person's risk of heart attack during the first hour after smoking marijuana can increase nearly five times.

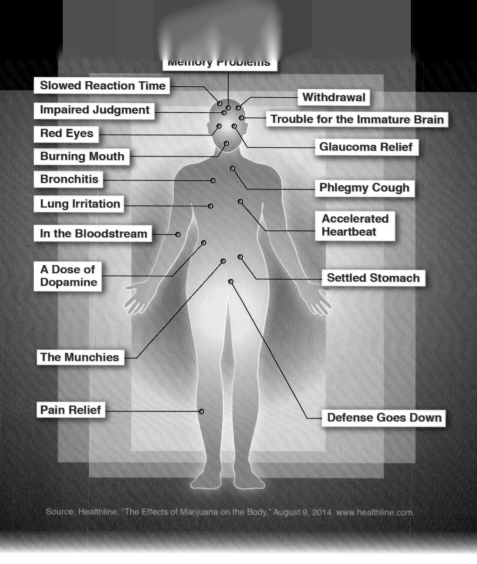

Memory Problems

Slowed Reaction Time

Impaired Judgment

Red Eyes

Burning Mouth

Bronchitis

Lung Irritation

In the Bloodstream

A Dose of Dopamine

The Munchies

Pain Relief

Withdrawal

Trouble for the Immature Brain

Glaucoma Relief

Phlegmy Cough

Accelerated Heartbeat

Settled Stomach

Defense Goes Down

Source: Healthline, "The Effects of Marijuana on the Body," August 9, 2014. www.healthline.com.

Marijuana smoke irritates the throat and lungs, sometimes causing the user to cough. Over time, particles and other chemicals in the smoke can damage the lungs. Smoking marijuana is linked to airway inflammation, increased airway resistance, and chronic bronchitis. It can also lower the user's immune system, increasing the likelihood of infection, pneumonia, and other respiratory illnesses.

Marijuana has several other physical effects. It can cause breathing passages to relax and enlarge. Blood vessels in the eyes expand, which makes a user's eyes appear bloodshot. Users may experience a head rush or dizziness when they stand, which increases the risk of fainting or injury from falls. Some feel as if their fingers and toes are cold, whereas others experience a very dry mouth. Marijuana can also slow a person's reaction time, which can affect his or her motor skills and coordination and impact athletic performance, impair driving skills, and increase injury risk.

How Marijuana Works in the Body

The human body actually has natural cannabinoid chemicals that work as neurotransmitters, sending chemical messages between nerve cells throughout the body's central nervous system. These neurotransmitters send messages to areas of the brain that control pleasure, memory, thinking, concentration, movement and coordination, the senses, and time perception. THC and other cannabinoid chemicals are similar to these natural neurotransmitters. When a user smokes a joint, THC and other cannabinoid chemicals in marijuana pass from his or her lungs into the bloodstream, where they are carried to the brain and other organs. If the marijuana is taken in food or drink, it is absorbed into the bloodstream through the user's digestive system.

Because THC is similar to the body's natural chemicals, it can attach to cannabinoid receptors on the neurons in these brain areas, which can activate the neurons and disrupt several mental and physical functions. This disruption causes the effects noticed by marijuana users as the drug's high. Disruption to the functioning of the hippocampus and orbitofrontal cortex—areas of the brain involved in forming new memories—can make it difficult for users to learn and perform complicated tasks while high. Disruption to the cerebellum and basal ganglia—areas of the brain that regulate balance, posture, coordination, and reaction—may explain why marijuana users have difficulty performing some physical tasks and experience slowed reaction times.

Impaired Driving

Drivers who get behind the wheel while high on marijuana may be putting themselves and others at risk. Marijuana impairs a driver's

Is Marijuana a Gateway Drug?

For years antimarijuana advocates have warned that marijuana is a gateway drug—a stepping-stone for users to more powerful and dangerous illicit drugs like cocaine and heroin. However, a 2015 study by researchers at New York University's Langone Medical Center's Department of Population Health suggests that marijuana may not be a gateway drug at all. Instead, the study authors suggest that teens who use marijuana do so for specific reasons, such as because they are bored or want to feel clarity. Researchers believe that these underlying reasons can motivate teens to try other drugs, not marijuana itself.

In the study, researchers reviewed data gathered from approximately fifteen thousand high school seniors surveyed between 2000 and 2011 who reported using marijuana in the previous twelve months. The researchers also analyzed the teens' self-reported use of other illicit drugs, including cocaine, heroin, and LSD. They found that teens who used marijuana because they were bored were 43 percent more likely to try cocaine and 56 percent more likely to try a hallucinogen other than LSD. Teens who used marijuana because they wanted to find clarity or understanding were 51 percent more likely to try a hallucinogen other than LSD. Yet the researchers also found that teens who said they used marijuana to experiment had a decreased risk of using any other illicit drugs. The researchers suggest that teens who are simply experimenting with marijuana, rather than using it to meet another need, are at low risk of using other drugs.

judgment, coordination, visual function, attention, and reaction time. Although some studies have found that marijuana has a lesser effect on drivers than alcohol, it still impairs driving performance. A 2015 study partially funded by the federal government found that people who used vaporized marijuana were more likely to weave within their lane than people who were sober. In the study, drivers with levels of 13 micrograms of THC per liter of blood showed increased weaving within a lane, similar to those driving with a breath alcohol level of 0.08, the legal threshold for drunk driving in many states. Researchers concluded that drivers under the influence of marijuana "may attempt to drive more cautiously to compensate for impairing effects."[21] Researchers also noted that smoking marijuana and drinking alcohol together enhanced the effects of both substances. Drivers who had used both weaved within lanes even if their blood levels of THC and alcohol were below the legal thresholds.

Driving while under marijuana's influence has been implicated as a factor in fatal car crashes. According to study published in 2014, fatal car crashes in which drivers tested positive for marijuana tripled in the United States between 1999 and 2010. Researchers from Columbia University gathered data from fatal car accidents in six states that included more than 23,500 drivers who died within one hour of a crash. They found that while alcohol contributed to about 40 percent of the fatal crashes, marijuana contributed to 12 percent, up from 4 percent in 1999. This increase in marijuana as a factor in fatal crashes occurred across all age groups for both males and females. "This study shows an alarming increase in driving under the influence of drugs, and, in particular, it shows an increase in driving under the influence of both alcohol and drugs,"[22] says Jan Withers, national president of Mothers Against Drunk Driving. Dr. Guohua Li, study coauthor and director of the Center for Injury Epidemiology and Prevention at Columbia University, noted that whereas a driver under the influence of alcohol had a thirteen times higher risk of a fatal crash than a sober driver, combining alcohol and marijuana increased the risk of a fatal crash twenty-four times over a sober person.

Effects on the Brain and IQ

Although many people regard marijuana as harmless, research shows that long-term heavy use of the drug, particularly if started at a young age, can have long-lasting effects. According to the NIDA, marijuana affects brain development. During adolescence, the brain is still forming and still building and streamlining connections. "Actually, in childhood our brain is larger," says Krista Lisdahl, director of the brain imaging and neuropsychology lab at the

University of Wisconsin–Milwaukee. "Then, during the teenage years, our brain is getting rid of those connections that weren't really used, and it prunes back. It actually makes the brain faster and more efficient."[23]

Using marijuana during this period of development may have long-term or permanent effects on a teen's thinking, memory, and learning functions. A growing number of studies show that using marijuana once a week or more can change the structure of the teen brain, particularly in areas that control memory and problem solving. For adolescents who use marijuana before age seventeen, this can lead to a decrease in verbal intelligence, verbal fluency, word recall, visual scanning ability, reaction time, and brain volume as adults.

A depressed teenage girl struggles to study her textbook. Teens who use marijuana are more likely to drop out of school and more likely to attempt suicide than those who do not use the drug.

In addition, heavy marijuana use as a teen can permanently lower a person's IQ. According to a 2012 study conducted in New Zealand, people who started smoking marijuana before age eighteen and were diagnosed as addicted to it by age thirty-eight experienced an average eight-point drop in IQ in early adulthood. Users who did not begin smoking marijuana until after age eighteen did not show a significant drop in IQ. "The effect of cannabis on IQ is really confined to adolescent users," says lead author Madeline Meier, a postdoctoral researcher at Duke University. "Our hypothesis is that we see this IQ decline in adolescence because the adolescent brain is still developing and if you introduce cannabis, it might interrupt these critical developmental processes."[24] The amount of marijuana smoked affected the study's results. Participants who smoked at least every day had the greatest drop in IQ. The younger they were when they started, the larger the drop in IQ. In addition, adults who smoked marijuana as teens performed worse in memory and decision-making tests than adults who did not smoke pot as teens.

Marijuana and Pregnancy

Marijuana use during pregnancy can have long-lasting effects on the baby. Some studies have found that babies exposed to marijuana before birth may have an increased risk of cognitive problems, attention-deficit disorder, anxiety, and depression. Marijuana can affect an unborn baby's brain development by interfering with how brain cells are wired and communicate with each other.

In 2014 researchers from Sweden and Austria looked at the effects marijuana had on mice and the brain tissue of human fetuses. They discovered that THC, marijuana's active ingredient, interferes with the formation of connections between nerve cells in the brain's cerebral cortex, the area that controls higher thinking skills and memory formation. The researchers identified a specific protein in nerve cells that is necessary for brain wiring. When exposed to THC, the brains of both human and mouse fetuses had lower levels of this protein than those that were not exposed to THC.

Difficulties in Daily Life

Marijuana use has also been associated with difficulties in daily life. Heavy marijuana users generally report lower life satisfaction, mental and physical health problems, relationship problems, and less success at school and work compared to their peers. Marijuana users are more likely to drop out of school, be late for or call in sick to work, or have accidents on the job than nonusers.

For teens, marijuana use can directly impact academic performance. "We see, if we look at actual grades, that chronic marijuana-using teens do have, on average, one grade point lower than their matched peers that don't smoke pot,"[25] says Lisdahl. Teens who use marijuana daily before age seventeen are more than 60 percent less likely to graduate from high school than their peers who do not use the drug, according to a 2014 study by researchers in Australia and New Zealand.

> "We see this IQ decline in adolescence because the adolescent brain is still developing and if you introduce cannabis, it might interrupt these critical developmental processes."[24]
>
> —Madeline Meier, a postdoctoral researcher at Duke University.

In the study, researchers analyzed the data of nearly four thousand participants, looking at the links between frequent marijuana use and several developmental outcomes. They found that teens who smoked marijuana daily were eighteen times more likely to become dependent on the drug, seven times more likely to attempt suicide, and eight times more likely to use other illegal drugs. "The results provide very strong evidence for a more direct relationship between adolescence cannabis use and later harm,"[26] says lead author Edmund Silins with the National Drug and Alcohol Research Centre at the University of New South Wales, Australia.

Link to Mental Illness

Regular marijuana use may also worsen the symptoms of existing mental illness or increase the chance that a teen develops mental illness in the future. According to a fact sheet from the

National Alliance on Mental Illness, "Using marijuana can directly worsen symptoms of anxiety, depression or schizophrenia through its actions on the brain."[27] People who smoke marijuana may be less likely to follow treatment plans for their mental illness, which can increase symptoms. Additionally, people at risk of developing schizophrenia, and who have close family members with severe mental illness, may be more likely to experience psychosis if they use marijuana. According to the alliance, regular users of marijuana are more likely to be diagnosed with schizophrenia at a younger age, are hospitalized more frequently for the illness, and are less likely to achieve a complete recovery even with treatment.

> "Using marijuana can directly worsen symptoms of anxiety, depression or schizophrenia through its actions on the brain."[27]
>
> —National Alliance on Mental Illness.

The amount of marijuana used, the age of the user, and family history are all factors that can influence whether marijuana plays a hand in the user developing mental illness. According to Dr. Christian Thurstone, an assistant professor of psychiatry at the University of Colorado–Denver, adolescents who use marijuana before age eighteen have up to a three times greater risk of developing permanent psychosis as adults, compared to peers who did not use the drug before age eighteen. Additionally, the more marijuana used, the greater the risk of developing psychotic symptoms.

Researchers are studying genes and the brain to understand how marijuana use affects psychosis. In a 2012 study, researchers at King's College London looked at a specific genetic variation in the AKT1 gene, which codes for an enzyme that affects how the neurotransmitter dopamine signals in the striatum, an area of the brain that is activated by dopamine when certain stimuli are present. The researchers found that a specific variation of AKT1 can increase the risk of developing psychosis in marijuana users. "We found that cannabis users who carry a particular variant in the AKT1 gene (rs2494732) had a two-fold increased probability of a psychotic disorder and this increased up to seven-fold if they used cannabis daily," say the study's authors. "Our findings help to explain why one cannabis user develops psychosis while his friends continue smoking without problems."[28] Earlier studies had found a link between marijuana use and a variation of the COMT gene, which controls an enzyme that breaks down dopamine, a neurotransmitter involved in schizophrenia.

However, recent research has offered some contradictions to these conclusions. In a 2015 study published by the American Psychological Association, chronic marijuana use by teen boys did not appear to be linked to physical or mental health issues later in life, such as depression, psychosis, or asthma. In the study, researchers from the University of Pittsburgh Medical Center and Rutgers University followed more than four hundred males from their teen years through their mid-thirties. "What we found was a little surprising," says lead researcher Jordan Bechtold. "There were no differences in any of the mental or physical health outcomes that we measured regardless of the amount or frequency of marijuana used during adolescence."[29]

Therapeutic Effects

Many people report that when used medicinally, as is legal in twenty-three states and the District of Columbia, marijuana can help manage a variety of diseases and conditions. Using marijuana therapeutically dates back as far as 2700 BCE, when the Chinese used cannabis tea to treat conditions such as gout, rheumatism, malaria, and poor memory. Today medical marijuana is used to reduce nausea and vomiting in cancer patients. It can also be used to decrease pain and inflammation and to ease muscle control problems. According to the American Academy of Neurology, medical marijuana can reduce the stiffness and muscle spasms sufferers of multiple sclerosis experience. It has also been suggested as a treatment for glaucoma, a disease in which increased pressure in the eyeball can cause blindness. Today the US Food and Drug Administration has approved two types of THC medications in pill form, although the plant form of marijuana has not been approved as a treatment.

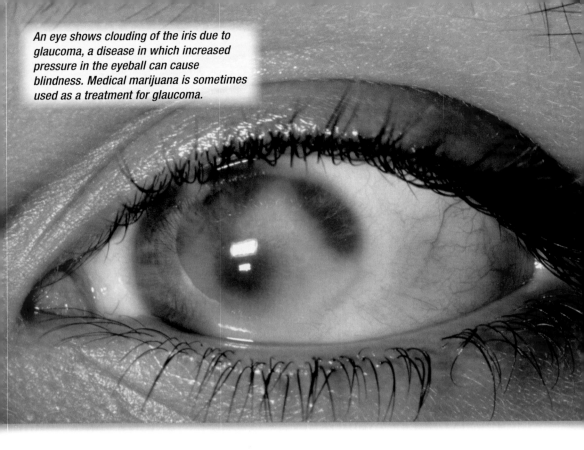

Cannabidiol (CBD) is a nonpsychoactive chemical in marijuana that also has therapeutic uses. CBD-based medicines reduce pain and inflammation and may be useful in controlling epileptic seizures. Because this type of medical marijuana does not target the brain's cannabinoid receptors, patients do not feel high when taking it.

One such patient is Addy Patrick, whose epileptic seizures began when she was only six months old. After testing, doctors discovered that a congenital brain malformation was causing the seizures. Before long, Addy was having three hundred seizures each day. Her parents followed her doctors' advice and heavily medicated Addy with anticonvulsants, which put her to sleep for most of the day.

Desperate to help her daughter, Addy's mother, Meagan, traveled to Colorado and met with parents whose children were taking a type of medical cannabis called Charlotte's Web, an oil high in CBD. She decided to try the experimental treatment for

Addy. Once Addy starting taking the oil, her seizures became less intense and decreased dramatically, to only one or two a day. Addy was also able to be weaned off some of her other medications, making her more alert and able to interact with friends and family. Meagan credits marijuana with her daughter's improvement. "We have Addy back again," says Meagan. "If I wasn't living though this, I don't know that I'd believe it myself. I don't feel like cannabis is a miracle cure. But I feel like it should be a tool in every neurologists' toolbox, all around the country."[30]

> "I don't feel like cannabis is a miracle cure. But I feel like it should be a tool in every neurologists' toolbox, all around the country."[30]
>
> —Meagan Patrick, the mother of a young girl who is using medical marijuana to treat epileptic seizures.

A Variety of Outcomes

For many people who smoke marijuana occasionally, the drug's effects are temporary and fade away after a few hours. With approved use under a doctor's supervision, medical marijuana has the potential to improve the lives of patients suffering from a number of diseases and symptoms. For others, especially those who begin using at a young age or become regular users, the effects of marijuana can be long lasting and permanent, affecting their health, mental state, academic performance, and relationships.

CHAPTER 3: How Addictive Is Marijuana?

For decades George of Raleigh, North Carolina, used marijuana to help him relax after a long day at work. Sometimes he smoked the drug every other day, and other times a few months would pass before he smoked again. Around age fifty George experienced some health problems and decided it was time to stop using marijuana. For him, quitting was easy. "There was no withdrawal," he says. "There was certainly no physical addiction. If you stopped eating chocolate, you would want to have chocolate again, but it's not really addictive."[31]

For millions of people like George, stopping marijuana use is no harder than giving up a favorite food—they are not physically or psychologically addicted to the drug. For other users, however, quitting marijuana can be much more difficult.

A Rare but Real Addiction

Although marijuana addiction is rare, it can be very real. According to the NIDA, approximately 9 percent of people who use marijuana will become dependent on it. The risk of addiction increases to about 17 percent for people who start using marijuana in their teens. Among those who use it daily, about 25 percent to 50 percent will become dependent on it. Beth, a nineteen-year-old from Missouri who smokes marijuana regularly, admits that she may be addicted. "When I can't find any weed, I get pretty anxious," she says. "I think I am addicted. Even though it's led me down some destructive paths, I feel so attached to marijuana that I can't see myself without it."[32]

When addicted, people cannot stop using a drug even if it interferes with many areas of life. They have difficulty controlling their use, regardless of consequences. If they try to stop, they experience withdrawal symptoms such as anxiety, irritability, restlessness, decreased appetite, weight loss, mood swings, and difficulty sleeping. Other, less common physical withdrawal symptoms of marijuana use include chills, stomach pain, shakiness, and sweating.

For Jake, a teen from New Jersey, marijuana addiction seriously impacted his life. A popular athlete and good student, Jake says that even in middle school, he was incredibly stressed out, putting pressure on himself to succeed in everything. When he was a high school freshman, Jake tried marijuana for the first time. "I felt this, like, unbelievable relief just from the world," he remembers. "I was on another planet and it was the most amazing thing to me. I didn't have to deal with reality." By the end of his freshman year, Jake was smoking pot every weekend. During his sophomore year he smoked every day. He was high when he played sports, did homework, and took tests.

Worried about his drug use, Jake's parents took him to see therapists and doctors but were told that since their son was still getting good grades and excelling on varsity sports teams, they should not be too concerned. Over time, however, Jake began stealing from his family to pay for marijuana. At first he would take money from his mom's purse. Later he stole sports memorabilia from his father and sold it, making $1,000 to $2,000 that he spent on drugs. "I kept trying to chase that first high, that first feeling of euphoria that I got when I smoked," Jake explains. "I think I started doing it so much that the effects stopped being so potent."[33]

> "When I can't find any weed, I get pretty anxious. I think I am addicted."[32]
>
> —Beth, a nineteen-year-old from Missouri who smokes marijuana regularly.

By the time Jake was a senior, his parents knew he was an addict. They confronted him and convinced him to seek help at a treatment center. Today Jake is in college and has been clean for months. Learning from past mistakes, he says that although smoking just one joint can feel great at first, "it stops being fun because I can't stop. I don't know how to stop."[34]

Marijuana's Increasing Potency

Over the years, marijuana's potency—the percentage of THC it contains—has been steadily increasing. The University of Mississippi tests the potency of all federally seized cannabis for the US government. Between 1985 and 2013, the average potency of all cannabis tested increased from 3.48 percent to 12.58 percent; that is, it nearly tripled in potency. Many are concerned that stronger cannabis will lead to more adverse effects, including addiction and overdose.

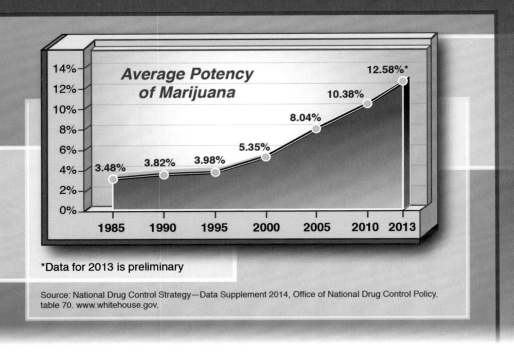

Average Potency of Marijuana

Year	Potency
1985	3.48%
1990	3.82%
1995	3.98%
2000	5.35%
2005	8.04%
2010	10.38%
2013	12.58%*

*Data for 2013 is preliminary

Source: National Drug Control Strategy—Data Supplement 2014, Office of National Drug Control Policy, table 70. www.whitehouse.gov.

Warning Signs

For many people marijuana use never becomes a problem; it doesn't interfere with performance at school or work or with personal relationships. This type of casual pot user is similar to a person who has a glass or two of wine a day without any problem. "That person, they're going to work, they're meeting their obligations, they're handling their responsibilities. We wouldn't call that person an addict,"[35] says Carl Hart, an associate professor of psychology at Columbia University.

For others marijuana use creates problems in daily life. Their performance at school, on sports teams, or at work may suffer if they are high all the time. Relationships with family and friends may be impacted because of regular drug use. In addition, users may get in trouble with school officials, employers, or even law enforcement because of their habit. Says Hart, "The bottom line is: Do you have a problem with drugs? A problem being defined by having disruptions in your psychosocial functioning. Disruptions in your occupational functioning. Your personal interactions and relationships. Your educational functioning. All these sort of things are disrupted. And that's what we call substance use disorder."[36]

Building a Tolerance

Over time using marijuana regularly can lead a person to build up a tolerance for the drug. When marijuana enters the brain, it boosts certain processes and functions far above normal levels. In order to protect itself, the brain learns to resist the drug's effects. Therefore, the next time a person uses marijuana, its effect is not as strong. To feel the same high, the person must smoke more and more. As tolerance builds, some people switch from smoking marijuana to consuming it in edible form or using highly concentrated extracts to achieve the same high.

As tolerance builds, it affects how the brain's reward system operates. Dopamine is an important neurotransmitter that regulates reward, motivation, and self-control. Drugs like marijuana work by stimulating dopamine signaling in the brain's main pleasure center. When dopamine is released, it activates the brain's reward centers, which makes taking the drug a pleasurable experience. However, as tolerance builds, the brain's reward centers respond less to dopamine signals.

A 2014 study by the NIDA found that the brains of marijuana abusers had a decreased response to dopamine. When given a chemical that causes dopamine levels to rise, study participants who used marijuana did not respond as strongly. "The problem isn't that they are releasing less dopamine, but that the dopamine stimulation in the brain is having a very attenuated effect," says Dr. Nora Volkow, director of the NIDA. "The brain doesn't know what to do with the dopamine. The dopamine signal is not being heard, not communicating properly downstream."[37] Volkow believes that marijuana use causes this decreased response to dopamine. Additionally, Volkow says that as tolerance builds, the brain shifts activity from the reward centers to other nearby brain regions involved in the formation of habits. For people who initially smoke marijuana because it is pleasurable, this switch can cause marijuana use to become an automatic habit or routine.

Dependence Forms

Once a person builds a tolerance to marijuana, continued use of the drug can lead to dependence. This happens as the brain attempts to return to a normal state over time. It compensates for the effects of marijuana by raising or lowering affected functions. For example, if marijuana lowers a user's heart rate, the brain will compensate by raising heart rate. Alternatively, the brain compensates by lowering a function—such as mood—that marijuana elevated. As a result, when the effects of marijuana wear off, the person's heart races, and he or she can become irritable or depressed—symptoms of withdrawal. "Daily use increases the risk of becoming dependent,"[38] says Roger Roffman, a professor emeritus at the University of Washington's School of Social Work.

> "Daily use increases the risk of becoming dependent."[38]
>
> —Roger Roffman, a professor emeritus at the University of Washington's School of Social Work.

Typically, a person has become dependent on marijuana if some sort of negative outcome occurs when he or she attempts to stop using. Although not as extreme as some other drugs, marijuana can cause withdrawal symptoms in regular, heavy users. "Withdrawal is the mirror-image of what the drug does," says Dr. Alex Stalcup, medical director of the New Leaf Treatment Center in Lafayette, California. "If cannabis makes you mellow, then you're irritable, grumpy."[39] Instead of feeling sedated, a person going through withdrawal may be unable to sleep. People who had increased appetite while using marijuana may now find that they have little appetite and are nauseous.

A Slow Addiction

Becoming addicted to marijuana is usually a slow process, one that takes months or even years. A person who has become addicted to

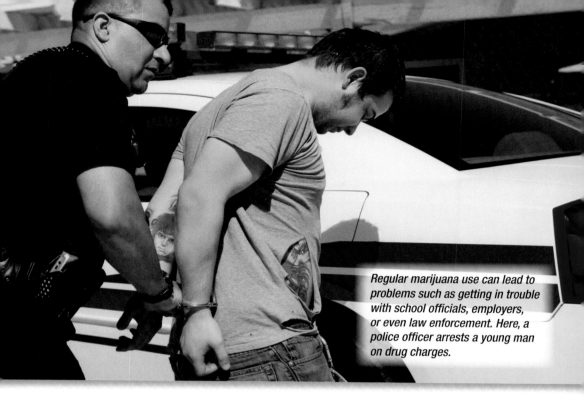

Regular marijuana use can lead to problems such as getting in trouble with school officials, employers, or even law enforcement. Here, a police officer arrests a young man on drug charges.

marijuana may not realize it at first. John Mariani, director of Columbia University's Substance Treatment and Research Service, says that marijuana addiction can be hard to recognize. "For people with alcohol, cocaine, opioid dependence, lots of bad stuff is happening to them that they don't want to have happen,"[40] he says. For example, they may end up in the emergency room after an overdose or be arrested and thrown in jail. For marijuana addicts, however, addiction is often much more subtle. "Often patients will have a philosophy that, 'This is something I choose to do. It's something I enjoy. It's something I benefit from.' And to some degree, that might be true,"[41] Mariani says. But as individuals slowly become addicted, they rationalize why it is all right to continue using the drug, even if they have started to experience negative consequences. They may not want to admit their addiction to others or even to themselves. As a result, they get stuck in a cycle of marijuana abuse.

Stalcup recommends a simple test for those who think they may be addicted to marijuana. He suggests that they try to stop using it for a defined period of time. "The basic question that we ask is, 'Okay, so you smoke pot, that's not the issue. Can

Increased Potency, Increased Addiction

Concerns are rising over the increased potency of contemporary marijuana and its potential to be more addictive and harmful, especially for teens who are in a critical period of brain development. According to data presented at the 2015 meeting of the American Chemical Society, today's marijuana has much higher levels of THC, the main psychoactive chemical that makes users feel high. "We've seen a big increase in marijuana potency compared to where it was 20 or 30 years ago," says Andy LaFrate, lab founder and director of research at Charas Scientific, who says today's marijuana is three times as strong as marijuana in the past. LaFrate added that some of the samples his lab has tested are even more potent in recent months. "As far as potency goes, it's been surprising how strong a lot of the marijuana is," says LaFrate. "We've seen potency values close to 30 percent THC, which is huge."

THC concentrations in marijuana plants can be increased by growers who crossbreed specific strains of the plant to get higher THC levels. Experts at the NIDA warn that higher concentrations of THC could increase the risk of an adverse reaction to marijuana and may also increase the risk of addiction for frequent users.

Quoted in CBS News, "Marijuana Far More Potent than It Used to Be, Tests Find," March 23, 2015. www.cbsnews.com.

you *not* smoke pot?'"[42] he says. If a person is not an addict, stopping marijuana use will not be a problem. However, if he or she is unable to stop, it is a strong sign that the person may be addicted.

Consequences of Addiction

Once addicted, the compelling desire to get high begins to influence a person's decision making, often at the expense of other areas of his or her life. Gantt Galloway, executive and research director of the New Leaf Treatment Center, explains that an addicted person does not make decisions rationally, in the same way a nonaddicted person does. An addict may place more emphasis on the immediate benefits rather than the long-term costs of using marijuana. "The person who's addicted . . . may not acknowledge that there are consequences of use—that they're not going to be as effective at work if they're stoned, that they're not going to be engaging with their family as well,"[43] says Galloway.

Relationships can suffer if addicted users decide that smoking pot is a higher priority than the needs of their partner, family, or friends. Lee, a twenty-four-year-old from Boston, explains how her boyfriend's addiction to marijuana affected their relationship. "He couldn't go to parties without knowing at what point in the night he'd get to go back to his place, or go somewhere else, and smoke," she says. "The only way he could get out of bed or get ready for the day (he was in school at the time) was to smoke. . . . There's a difference between the casual stoner who prefers smoking to drinking and the guy who can't have normal social behavior."[44] Fed up with his behavior, Lee eventually broke up with her boyfriend.

For Jake, his addiction to marijuana caused problems at home. His brother Ben says that while Jake was addicted, their house seemed to have no energy, no love, and no feelings of happiness; he and his parents just watched and worried about Jake's relentless addiction to marijuana and other drugs. "The lengths my brother went to that I personally witnessed were pretty out there. It wasn't normal behavior,"[45] says Ben. In testimony before the New York City Council in 2011, Max Schwartzberg, a substance abuse therapist and former marijuana addict, described how marijuana affected his relationships: "It's hard to hold a girlfriend's hand when you're always rolling a blunt. It's hard to be a son when you're stealing money from your mother. And it's even harder to be an older brother when you've been stoned his entire life."[46]

Addiction can also have negative consequences at work or at school. Many employers have zero-tolerance policies for drug use and require employees to take random drug tests. Those who test positive for marijuana use can be fired. Even in Colorado, where

> "The person who's addicted . . . may not think through or may not acknowledge that there are consequences of use—that they're not going to be as effective at work if they're stoned, that they're not going to be engaging with their family as well."[43]
>
> —Gantt Galloway, executive and research director of the New Leaf Treatment Center.

medical and recreational marijuana is legal, the state's Supreme Court ruled that employers have the right to fire employees for using marijuana. For example, in 2015 the Colorado Supreme Court ruled that national satellite TV provider Dish Network acted legally when it fired employee Brandon Coats, a call center representative, after he tested positive for marijuana. The court ruled that although Colorado allows the use of medical marijuana, Dish had the right to fire Coats because marijuana is still illegal under federal law.

For some people marijuana addiction can lead to trouble with the law. Some people are arrested if they are caught with the illegal substance. Even in states where marijuana is legal, driving while high is a crime. Some states have a zero-tolerance policy for marijuana, whereas others have set blood test limits for marijuana similar to blood alcohol limits for drunk driving or use other tests to determine a driver's impairment. In Colorado, where recreational marijuana was legalized in 2012, approximately one in every eight citations issued by the Colorado State Patrol in 2014 for impaired driving involved suspected marijuana use.

Risk Factors for Addiction

To date, scientists are unsure what causes one person to become addicted to marijuana while another does not, but they believe that certain factors may increase a person's risk. Age and frequency of use are two factors that influence who becomes addicted to marijuana. Users who start smoking pot as teens and those who use it daily are more likely to become addicted than those who start later in life and use it only occasionally.

Genetics likely also play a role in who becomes addicted to marijuana. Addiction is more common in some families than others. People with parents or siblings who are addicted to drugs or alcohol may have an increased risk of becoming addicted themselves. Studies of twins show that identical twins raised in different environments are more likely to both have addictions than fraternal twins raised apart, suggesting that there is a genetic component to addiction.

Experiencing trauma, particularly sexual trauma at a young age, may also increase a person's risk of addiction. "We have long known that childhood adversity, and in particular sexual abuse, is associated with the development of cannabis dependence,"[47] says Ryan Bogdan, an assistant professor of psychological and brain sciences at Washington University in St. Louis. Trauma, combined with a genetic predisposition, may explain why some people become dependent on marijuana while others do not.

This was the finding of a 2015 study from Washington University in St. Louis, in which researchers examined genetic data from more than fifteen hundred marijuana users who self-reported sexual abuse as children. The researchers found an association between certain genetic variations and the likelihood that participants became dependent on marijuana. "As we expected, childhood sexual abuse was overall associated with individuals reporting a greater number of cannabis dependence symptoms,"[48] says Caitlin E. Carey, a PhD student working with Bogdan. In addition,

Teens who are depressed, have a chaotic home life, or struggle in school may turn to marijuana as an escape from their problems.

Marijuana Versus Alcohol

For years people have debated which substance is more harmful—alcohol or marijuana. In research published in the journal *Scientific Reports* in 2015, researchers compared the risk of death associated with the typical recreational use of several substances: marijuana, alcohol, tobacco, heroin, cocaine, ecstasy, methamphetamine, diazepam, amphetamine, and methadone. They found that alcohol was the deadliest substance, followed by tobacco, ecstasy, and meth.

Marijuana was found to be the safest—approximately 114 times less deadly than alcohol. Researchers said that their findings suggest that the danger of marijuana may have been overestimated, whereas the danger of alcohol may be underestimated. Even though few deaths have been linked to marijuana overdose, however, some experts warn that chronic marijuana use has been linked to lung problems, addiction, and worrisome changes in the developing teen brain.

Carey explains that researchers found a variation of a gene that appears to provide some sort of protection against the development of cannabis dependence. Participants who had that gene variation did not show an association between cannabis dependence and childhood sexual abuse.

Another factor that may influence who develops a marijuana addiction is the environment in which people live. Teens living in a chaotic home situation or who are struggling at school may turn to marijuana because it is pleasurable and takes them away from their problems. These teens may have a higher risk of using the drug and, over time, of becoming addicted.

Having a mental illness can also put a person at a higher risk of developing an addiction to marijuana. According to Stalcup, approximately 50 to 60 percent of marijuana abusers that his clinic treats have an underlying mental illness such as depression, anxiety, post-traumatic stress disorder, or schizophrenia. "Mental health is a huge risk factor for addiction," says Stalcup, adding:

> Drugs work very well, at first, for mentally ill people. If you're anxious, it'll go away with a couple of hits, a beer. It's like magic. But then, the tolerance sets in. So, not only

do they need to drink more to relieve the anxiety, but every single time they try to stop, the underlying anxiety comes back worse. We conceptualize it as a biological trap. It works at first, it turns on you, it stops working, and then you still have a problem.[49]

Protecting Against Addiction

Although several factors increase the risk of marijuana addiction, having close family ties may mitigate risk factors for addiction. According to Hart, when people are closely connected to friends and family members, they are less likely to become addicted to marijuana. In addition, people who feel as if they have more choices in life tend not to become addicted to pot. Galloway explains:

Most of us have a lot of choice in life of things that make us feel good. Those who have fewer choices, who perhaps don't have as rich a set of social interactions because their family life is difficult or because they have emotional problems that are stopping them from forming close friendships . . . those people may find drugs such as marijuana more attractive and be at greater risk for addiction.[50]

Most people who use marijuana will not become addicted. For those who do, the addiction can have negative consequences, impacting health, relationships, school, and work. Because using marijuana has become more socially and legally accepted, its potential for abuse may surprise some people. "The belief that marijuana is safer is increasing . . . and so the attitudes are changing," says Bridget Grant, laboratory chief of the epidemiology and biometry lab at the National Institute on Alcohol Abuse and Alcoholism. "But we know there are a lot of harms that are related to it, and that includes addiction."[51]

CHAPTER 4: Challenges of Treatment and Recovery

Seventeen-year-old Jynessa from Colorado struggles with marijuana addiction. "It's the same as if your body is telling you that you are hungry, how your stomach growls," says Jynessa. "It just feels that I need to smoke weed. I'm craving it right now. I can feel it." Jynessa was a straight-A student and athlete when she first got high on marijuana at age fourteen. She liked the feeling and started hanging out with a new group of friends and smoking pot on a regular basis. "I just liked being high," Jynessa says. "I got used to seeing my face being high, how I looked being high. I just liked the whole ritual. I was like, 'alright I'm going to wake up. I'm going to smoke some weed. I'm going to go to school. People are going to know that I'm high.' It seemed cool."[52] Jynessa also liked the way marijuana made her feel; it shielded her from pressure at school and at home.

By her sophomore year, Jynessa was smoking marijuana a lot. Before long, her drug use began to affect her school work and athletics. When she stopped practicing softball to get high, her performance suffered and she ended up quitting the team. In addition, she cut class to smoke weed, which led to failing an honors class. "That's when I was like, 'I'm really unmotivated.' I really don't even want to play my favorite sport in the world that I played since I was 6? I'm really not playing that because of weed?"[53]

One day, after she smoked marijuana and then returned to school, security guards confronted her. At first she denied her drug use, but eventually she confessed. She had become addicted to marijuana. To get help, Jynessa agreed to enter Adams City High's Encompass treatment program, an eight-week pilot program to treat teen drug abuse. Although she was hesitant at first, Jynessa soon realized that the program's individualized therapy was helping. She learned how to understand the feelings that made her crave marijuana. She says that treatment is helping her understand why she used marijuana and how to recognize negative thoughts and turn them into positive ones. She has also taken up activities such as drawing to distract her when she feels the urge to get high.

So far, treatment has helped Jynessa reduce her drug use, but she still struggles with giving it up entirely. "I know I'm addicted,"[54] Jynessa says, recognizing that she still faces many challenges because of marijuana. Still, with continued treatment, she hopes to realize her plans of going to college after high school and studying graphic design.

Withdrawing from Marijuana

Across the United States approximately 4.2 million people aged twelve or older had a marijuana use disorder in the previous year, according to the 2014 National Survey on Drug Use and Health. These people have difficulty controlling their marijuana use, often at the expense of other areas of their lives. Strained relationships with family and friends, poor performance at school or work, and even trouble with the law are significant negative consequences that those addicted to marijuana face.

Once addicted to marijuana, users can experience withdrawal symptoms if they decide to stop. Typically, withdrawal symptoms are temporary and peak a few days after stopping use; they generally last about two weeks. Some withdrawal symptoms, however, can reoccur for up to two years as the brain tries to return to its normal state. Withdrawal—both experiencing it and fearing it—poses a challenge to treatment for and recovery from marijuana abuse.

Long-term marijuana users can experience physical withdrawal, which includes nausea and decreased appetite. They may also become irritable and have trouble sleeping. Some people report having nightmares that can continue for several months, as well as cravings for marijuana. Psychologically, withdrawal can trigger feelings of anxiety and depression. "I have seen both men and women cry, on and off daily, literally for

A marijuana pipe and dried marijuana leaves are shown. Marijuana addiction can lead to withdrawal symptoms such as nausea, irritability, sleeping difficulties, anxiety, and depression for those who stop using it.

many months after they've stopped smoking pot," says Lynn O'Connor, a clinical psychologist who studies depression, anxiety disorders, and addiction. O'Connor, who has worked with numerous patients experiencing withdrawal, describes this state in the following way:

> This depression is defined by the recovering addict experiencing an intense, almost shattering drop in self-confidence and self-esteem. Living under a dark cloud of foreboding, they find themselves ruminating about people they believe they might have harmed during their active addiction. Often, the harms they believe they've committed, are entirely imaginary. But they suffer, and most start believing: "this is the way I am, I'll have to smoke pot or feel like this" instead of realizing that everything they are thinking and feeling is a function of withdrawal from marijuana, and that it will stop at some point.[55]

The prospect of facing withdrawal discourages some people from stopping their marijuana use. Others try stopping for a short period but ultimately relapse. This is what happened to Jason, a forty-three-year-old from Seattle, who never thought it was possible to become addicted to marijuana. Although he smoked pot every day for ten years, he thought he could stop whenever he wanted. When he decided to quit for health reasons, he began to experience withdrawal. "For the first couple days, I didn't feel much different," he says. "The third day, I was, oddly enough, very hungry. I became very, very hungry, like I couldn't get enough food in." In addition, "I started having very extreme dreams, very detailed, increasingly intense, bizarre stories." Jason says that he felt as if "an essential nutrient was missing" when he did not smoke marijuana. When Jason's symptoms continued for three weeks, he started to smoke pot again. "I was actually surprised, the level of dependence," he says. "I was kind of shocked and surprised that [the withdrawal symptoms] were so pronounced—more like a psych med than stopping coffee and being curmudgeonly and tired."[56]

> "I have seen both men and women cry, on and off daily, literally for many months after they've stopped smoking pot."[55]
>
> —Lynn O'Connor, a clinical psychologist who studies depression, anxiety disorders, and addiction.

Success with Therapy

Once a person has detoxified and removed all marijuana from his or her system, he or she must learn how to avoid using for the long term. People who become addicted to marijuana have usually developed habits and rituals around their drug use. If left untreated, they are likely to slip back into the behaviors that led to marijuana use in the first place. Therefore, they must learn new habits and behaviors that enable them to avoid marijuana and other drugs.

Several types of psychotherapy have proved successful in treating marijuana addiction. Psychotherapy can take place in an outpatient or inpatient program. In either setting, therapy generally involves some sort of motivational approach that is combined with teaching patients effective coping skills. Therapies include motivation enhancement therapy, cognitive behavioral therapy, and contingency management.

Motivation enhancement therapy (MET) is a counseling approach that helps patients stop feeling ambivalent about stopping marijuana use and seeking treatment. MET attempts to internally motivate the patient to *want* to stop using marijuana, rather than just following a counselor through treatment steps. MET has been used successfully for marijuana, nicotine, and alcohol addictions. This therapy typically begins with an initial assessment session, followed by two to four treatment sessions with a therapist. In these sessions, the therapist and patient talk about strategies to cope with situations that are high risk for triggering drug use. The therapist monitors the patient's progress, assesses the success of strategies being used, and encourages the patient to continue his or her commitment to change and abstain from marijuana. Typically, MET is most effective for patients already in treatment, rather than for people who are still using pot.

In many cases MET is used in tandem with cognitive behavioral therapy (CBT) to treat marijuana addiction. CBT is a form of psychotherapy that teaches patients the skills they need to stop drug use. In CBT, patients learn strategies that help them identify and correct behaviors that led to drug use, which improves their self-control. For example, a patient may learn relaxation techniques such as deep breathing to manage stress and anxiety instead of lighting up a joint. A central part of CBT is that it teaches patients how to anticipate situations that trigger drug use and gives them coping strategies that do not involve turning to marijuana. Patients learn to recognize cravings and identify high-risk situations for drug use. They learn strategies to help them avoid tempting situations and cope with drug cravings without getting high.

Contingency management (CM) gives patients rewards of increasing value to reinforce positive behaviors such as abstaining from marijuana. For example, patients can earn a voucher for every drug test they pass. The voucher may have a monetary value that can be redeemed for food, movie passes, or other goods and services. In the beginning the voucher value is low but increases as patients pass more and more drug tests. Another form

Dependence Versus Addiction

Although dependence and addiction often occur together, not everyone who is dependent on marijuana is addicted to the drug. Dependence on marijuana is a physical condition in which people need the drug to feel physically OK. They may need marijuana to help them sleep or to reduce nausea. Moreover, they will experience specific physical symptoms when they stop using marijuana. This physical dependence occurs from chronic use.

Addiction to marijuana can be understood as compulsive drug use. An addicted person continues to use marijuana despite harmful consequences, at the expense of people and activities that he or she used to enjoy. Those with a marijuana addiction become consumed with using the drug and getting high. They think about marijuana most of the time and forgo other priorities in their life so they can get high. They are unable to stop using even if it causes problems at school, at work, and in relationships.

of CM includes chances to win cash prizes for passing drug tests, attending counseling sessions, and other positive behaviors. In both forms of CM, if a patient relapses into negative behaviors and drug use, the rewards are removed.

For adolescent marijuana abusers, family behavior therapy (FBT) may be used in addition to individual therapy. FBT addresses substance abuse problems along with co-occurring problems such as conduct disorders, depression, and family conflict. In FBT, therapists engage the patient and at least one other family member, typically a parent. Together they learn behavioral strategies and skills to improve the home environment. During each session, the family reviews behavioral goals with the therapist, and rewards are provided when the goals are achieved. These therapies attempt to teach the addict and family members skills to help discourage marijuana use.

Lack of Medication

For some drug addictions—such as addiction to opiates—certain medications have proved useful for treatment. However, no such medication has been shown to help treat marijuana addiction.

Scientists hope that research into addiction will lead to effective and safe medical treatments. For example, some promising research involves medications that inhibit the body's natural cannabinoids and interact with cannabinoid receptors to nullify the effects of THC.

In 2015 the National Institutes of Health dedicated $3 million to fund and fast-track the development of drugs to treat marijuana addiction. The agency plans to award $3 million to fund three projects to develop drugs that reduce marijuana abuse. "Cannabis use is an increasing public health concern in the United States that requires immediate attention," reads the government's grant proposal, issued in May 2015. "Given the high prevalence of marijuana use and its associated disorders and the large number of people who seek treatment, there is a critical need to discover and develop safe and effective treatments."[57]

Some medications can help people manage uncomfortable withdrawal symptoms, which in turn may help them avoid relapsing. For example, antidepressant medications may ease symptoms of depression or anxiety. Other medications may reduce nausea or help a person sleep. Some studies are focusing on using existing or developing new medications that help with the sleep problems that arise during marijuana withdrawal. These medications can be used to manage withdrawal symptoms for a few weeks until the symptoms begin to ease.

Barriers to Successful Treatment

Because marijuana addiction develops over a long period of time, it can be very hard to treat. In addition, several barriers make it difficult for addicted people to achieve long-term recovery.

One of the most imposing barriers to recovery is the belief that marijuana addiction is not a serious problem. Many users believe that they cannot become physically addicted to marijuana and therefore do not subscribe to the idea that they have a problem that could benefit from professional help. As a result, relatively few seek treatment. "I thought marijuana addiction was a joke," says eighteen-year-old Rocco Mastriona, who has been in two residential programs for substance abuse, one called Arapahoe

More Teens Treated for Marijuana than for Other Drugs

Although treatment for marijuana use among teens is declining, more teens are treated for problems with marijuana than for any other substance. This is according to a 2015 report that looked at drug treatment program admissions for adolescents between the ages of twelve and seventeen. The total number of marijuana-related admissions fell from 101,378 in 2003 to 77,062 in 2013. Even so, the number of admissions to treatment programs for other commonly abused drugs was far lower than for marijuana for that age group.

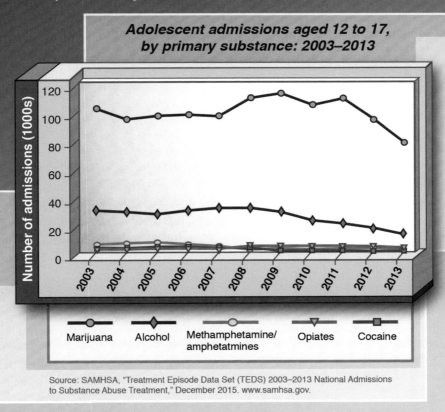

Adolescent admissions aged 12 to 17, by primary substance: 2003–2013

Source: SAMHSA, "Treatment Episode Data Set (TEDS) 2003–2013 National Admissions to Substance Abuse Treatment," December 2015. www.samhsa.gov.

House. "My primary drug was heroin, but marijuana played a big role in my relapse after the first time I left Arapahoe House. I thought if I stayed away from pills and heroin and just smoked weed, I'd be OK."[58]

Of the people who do seek treatment for marijuana addiction, long-term recovery success rates are low. According to the US National Library of Medicine, marijuana addiction recovery

Support Groups

For long-term treatment, some people turn to support groups to help them avoid marijuana. Support groups help addicts deal with the daily challenges of living without marijuana. People who are going through the same challenges can provide invaluable support and advice. For many recovering marijuana addicts, participating in a support group is a key part of maintaining a drug-free life.

One support group, Marijuana Anonymous (MA), is a 12-step program modeled after Alcoholics Anonymous. Members have a common desire to abstain from marijuana. New members are assigned to a sponsor who has been clean for at least a year. This person helps recovering addicts deal with cravings and challenges as they occur. As a first step, addicts admit that they are powerless to stop using marijuana and that they have a problem. Members work through the following steps, thinking critically about decisions they have made in their lives and making amends to people their addictive behavior has harmed.

MA members regularly attend meetings, where they listen to speakers, participate in group discussions, study literature, and celebrate staying clean. Meetings offer them a safe place to talk about the reasons they used marijuana and learn how to manage daily stresses without the drug.

success rates ranged between just 9 percent and 29 percent. The majority of users return to old habits. According to Rehabilitation International, only half of people who enter a treatment program for marijuana abuse will stay clean after two weeks. Of those who complete a treatment program, about 50 percent will return to marijuana within one year.

The severity and type of withdrawal symptoms may increase the risk of relapse in some marijuana users. According to research from the National Cannabis Prevention and Information Centre in New South Wales, Australia, dependent users who experienced physical tension, sleep problems, anxiety, depression, mood swings, and loss of appetite were more likely to relapse than users who experienced hot flashes, fatigue, or night sweats during withdrawal. The researchers hope that these findings may help therapists improve counseling and treatment strategies. "Tailoring treatments to target withdrawal symptoms contributing to functional impairment during a quit attempt may improve treatment outcomes,"[59] says lead researcher David Allsop.

Recovery Is Not Easy, but Possible

Marijuana addiction is a complicated and chronic condition. Many patients need a long-term care approach that is customized to their changing needs. Although it may be difficult, recovery is possible. "Every addicted patient I've seen has wanted to get into recovery," says O'Connor. "They may not all know it at first, they may not know it consciously, but they want recovery."[60]

The journey to recovery is not always easy, as one anonymous marijuana user reports. "Few, if any, of us who struggle with addiction can get sober alone," he says, and shares the following experience:

> "I thought marijuana addiction was a joke. My primary drug was heroin, but marijuana played a big role in my relapse."[58]
>
> —Rocco Mastriona, an eighteen-year-old marijuana addict who has been in two residential programs for substance abuse.

I would "quit" every morning, sure that I would be able stay clean for the day. But every night, after some small success or disappointment, I would find a reason to call my dealer or scrape up what was left from the day before. I learned the meaning of desperation, as only the addicted know it. I could not bear to use nor could I bear to live without using. I needed to quit but was unable to do so on my own. I struggled to keep my public, successful, professional persona separate from my private, desperate, addicted self. These two sides constantly felt as if they were collapsing inward.[61]

Eventually, he reached out to a therapist for help, hoping to hear that he was overreacting and did not have a serious problem. The therapist told him that he was addicted to marijuana but also that help was available. He decided to enter treatment and start his journey to recovery, which has been tough at times. "I was consumed by shame and a sense of loss in the early days," he says. "I had terrible dreams of using and of getting caught. But as time passed, I emerged from addiction into a new life. . . . I became proud of passing my weekly drug tests," he says. He also joined a 12-step recovery program in his community and learned to communicate and work with people from all backgrounds and personalities. As a result, he reports being in a much better place, although he continues to work on his recovery every day. "I'm a loving and involved father, a devoted son, and a valued friend. I have a loving relationship with a wonderful woman who supports my recovery. I have a life and a career second to none. I have learned to be grateful for these many blessings. I have found some measure of serenity."[62]

> "I had terrible dreams of using and of getting caught. But as time passed, I emerged from addiction into a new life. . . . I became proud of passing my weekly drug tests."[62]
>
> —A marijuana user.

CHAPTER 5: Preventing Marijuana Use

For some people, there are no long-term effects or consequences of occasional marijuana use. For others, especially those who begin using as adolescents or become regular users, marijuana can have long-lasting and permanent effects, impacting health, mental state, academic performance, and relationships. Regular use of marijuana can also lead to addiction. Therefore, preventing marijuana use at an early age can help reduce addiction and other serious effects of use.

A Risky Time—Adolescence

Trying new things and taking risks is a normal part of teen development. During these years, teens face many transitions, including graduating from elementary to middle school, or middle to high school, or possibly moving to a new town. All of these changes present social and academic challenges. Many teens feel pressure to fit in and conform to what others are wearing or doing. These stresses may cause some teens to experiment with marijuana.

At the same time teens are adapting to social changes, many are exposed to cigarettes, alcohol, and drugs like marijuana for the first time. By the time they enter high school, teens may find marijuana is readily available. Their peers may be using it before and after school, and in various social situations. As a result, some decide to try it. Some do so to fit in with friends or not to feel left out. Others think that smoking pot will make them seem cool or make them feel more relaxed at parties.

Adolescence is a critical time for preventing marijuana use. According to SAMHSA's 2013 National Survey on Drug Use and Health, an estimated 2.4 million people aged twelve or older used marijuana for the first time within the past year. More than half of these first-time users—1.4 million people—were younger than age eighteen. Research has shown that using marijuana while the brain is still developing can have long-term effects and increase the chance of developing an addiction. Therefore, programs that prevent teen marijuana use can reduce overall rates of addiction and other negative consequences.

Research-Based Prevention Programs

Over the years, researchers have studied how drug abuse begins and how it progresses. They have found that many factors can increase a person's risk for drug abuse, whereas different factors can protect against drug abuse. These risk and protective factors affect children and teens differently at various points in their lives. For example, family risk factors (such as a lack of parental involvement) have a greater effect on a younger child, whereas hanging out with friends who use marijuana is a greater risk factor in adolescence. In addition, not everyone has the same risk factors; a risk factor for one person may not be a risk factor for another.

Using current scientific evidence, research-based prevention programs have successfully reduced early use of tobacco, alcohol, and illicit drugs, including marijuana, by enhancing protective factors and reducing risk factors. These programs focus on reducing risk by intervening early in a child's development to strengthen his or her protective factors. For example, children who exhibit aggressive behavior have a higher risk of marijuana use later in life. This risk factor can be reduced with interventions that help children develop appropriate and positive behaviors and develop self-control (a protective factor). If not addressed, aggressive behavior can lead to academic failure, social difficulties, and additional risk factors, which further increase a child's risk for marijuana use later in life.

Effective research-based prevention programs can be used in the family, in schools, and in communities. Such programs fall into several categories. Universal programs are designed and used for general populations, such as the entire student body at a high school. Selective programs target groups that are at higher risk

A teenage girl smokes a joint at a party. Many teens decide to try marijuana in order to fit in, seem cool, or feel more relaxed at parties.

of marijuana abuse, such as children of drug abusers. Indicated prevention programs are programs used for people who have already experimented with drugs.

Family Focus

Research has shown that parents play a critical role in preventing a child's marijuana use later in life. According to a 2012 study from North Carolina State University and several partner institutions, parental involvement is more important than school environment for preventing or limiting marijuana and alcohol use by children. In the study, researchers examined data from more than ten thousand students, along with their parents, teachers, and school administrators. They compared how "family social capital" and "school social capital" affected the likelihood of marijuana and alcohol use. The study defined family social capital as parent-child bonds, including

Don't Be a Lab Rat

Although many community programs have been successful in preventing marijuana use, others have had mixed results. In 2014 Colorado public health officials launched the Don't Be a Lab Rat campaign, which compared pot smokers to laboratory animals. Along with television commercials, the campaign placed three 8-by-12-foot (2.4-by-3.7-m) cages in public spaces to warn against the dangers of marijuana use. The cages feature messages such as, "Subjects needed. Must be a teenager. Must smoke weed. Must have 8 IQ points to spare."

Many in Colorado's legal pot industry and some young people criticized the campaign, calling it a scare tactic. The city of Boulder, in fact, declined an offer from the state to set up a cage display. City officials explained that although they supported marijuana education, they did not believe the Lab Rat campaign was an appropriate way to communicate the message. However, Colorado public health officials defended the campaign, saying that it was intended to start a conversation about marijuana use and send the message that using marijuana can be harmful. "Whether you hate it or love it, or are somewhere in between, at least you have people talking about it," says Larry Wolk, chief medical officer and executive director of the Colorado Department of Public Health & Environment.

Quoted in Dan Frosch, "Colorado 'Lab Rat' Campaign Warns Teens of Pot Use," *Wall Street Journal*, October 5, 2014. www.wsj.com.

trust, open communication, and active engagement in a child's life. In comparison, school social capital measured the school's positive environment for learning, student involvement in extracurricular activities, teacher morale, and whether teachers were able to address individual student needs.

For both marijuana and alcohol use, researchers found that students with high levels of family social capital were less likely to have used marijuana or alcohol than students with high school social capital but low family social capital. "Parents play an important role in shaping the decisions their children make when it comes to alcohol and marijuana," says Dr. Toby Parcel, a sociology professor at North Carolina State University. "To be clear, school programs that address alcohol and marijuana use are definitely valuable, but the bonds parents form with their children are more important. Ideally, we can have both."[63]

Because the family is such a key protective factor in preventing marijuana abuse, programs that focus on the family can be very effective at strengthening protective factors in young children. These programs teach parents better communication skills and family management skills. They also teach appropriate styles of discipline and how to be firm and consistent when enforcing family rules.

In Greensburg, Pennsylvania, Lynna Thomas has a yellow magnet clip on her refrigerator. It holds concept cards from weekly sessions of the Strengthening Families Program, which she attended in 2014 with her middle school–aged daughter. "The cards are year-round visual reminders of important things and tools learned in the program for communicating and keeping your family strong,"[64] Thomas says. Developed in 1997, the Strengthening Families Program is a skills-building program for parents, youth, and families that is used across the country. In Westmoreland County, where Thomas lives, the program targets fifth and sixth graders. It teaches students how to make healthy decisions about substance abuse and behavioral issues, which commonly arise at that age.

> "Parents play an important role in shaping the decisions their children make when it comes to alcohol and marijuana."[63]
>
> —Dr. Toby Parcel, a professor of sociology at North Carolina State University.

According to Westmoreland County program coordinator Patty Graff, the program's success relies on its ability to improve relationships and decrease family conflict. Says Graff:

> Kids tend to stop talking to adults at that point in their life; it's such a huge, emotional time for them with all of the hormonal changes that start to kick in. The program premise is: If you lay a good foundation with communication at home, the child will have a protective anchor—someone they can go to who truly cares for them and will support them—while they try to figure out the world.[65]

A teenage girl works on a laptop while her family members look on. Research has shown that active parental involvement plays a vital role in preventing teens from using marijuana.

Program participants attend weekly sessions that are run by trained facilitators. After a meal, sessions begin with parents and children in separate groups. They work on skills such as understanding the other person's point of view. Children discuss peer pressure and stress, and parents talk about subjects such as house rules, consequences, and how children use negative behavior for control and independence. Then families gather back together to practice the skills they have learned. The program teaches those in both groups to put their own thoughts aside for the moment so that they can stop and really listen to each other.

School-Based Programs

School-based prevention programs target children in the school environment. They aim to boost students' protective factors against marijuana use by improving their social and academic skills, peer relationships, self-control, and coping skills. "Sadly, now more than ever school-based drug-prevention programs are a necessity," says Chancellor J. Keith Motley of the University of Massachusetts–Boston, which in 2015 evaluated the implementation of an antidrug program in Boston public schools. "Statistics show that 9 out of 10 people with addiction started using substances before they turned 18. We hope that by focusing on adolescents before they are exposed to drugs and alcohol, we can diminish the risk of addiction, and increase the likelihood of success in school and in college."[66]

School-based prevention programs can take many forms. School programs may distribute materials that include information about marijuana that correct the idea that "everyone" is smoking pot. They may feature the personal stories of former addicts or the experiences of relatives of marijuana addicts who share how the drug negatively impacted their families. Some programs also use science to explain what marijuana does to the developing brain. These programs are most effective if they are introduced early, says Robert LaChausse, a psychologist and professor at California Baptist University. "Each year that you delay drug use among teenagers you increase the odds that they will never use drugs,"[67] he says.

In Boston, Massachusetts, Mayor Marty Walsh announced in 2015 that a prevention program, Too Good for Drugs, would be implemented for seventh graders in all Boston public schools. The program uses ten one-hour sessions with trained prevention professionals to teach students skills for good decision making and resisting peer pressure. It will also help them build communication skills and pursue healthy relationships with others. According to Walsh, "It emphasizes the pertinent information Boston youth will need to understand the negative consequences of alcohol and drug use."[68] John McGahan, president of the Gavin Foundation, a substance

> "We hope that by focusing on adolescents before they are exposed to drugs and alcohol, we can diminish the risk of addiction, and increase the likelihood of success in school and in college."[66]
>
> —Chancellor J. Keith Motley of the University of Massachusetts–Boston.

abuse treatment, education, and prevention agency that will implement the program in Boston, says that the earlier students learn these skills, the more effective the prevention program will be. "We want to give them the tools they need now, so that they won't make a bad choice,"[69] he says.

Community Efforts

Communities around the country have partnered with civic, religious, law enforcement, and other organizations to prevent marijuana and other drug use. Community programs often coordinate prevention efforts with those undertaken by other entities—such as schools, media, and religious groups—so that a consistent message is heard. Community prevention efforts include developing policies and regulations, conducting mass media campaigns, and launching broad community awareness programs, among other efforts.

In 2015, for example, the Colorado Department of Public Health & Environment launched a new youth marijuana education and prevention program aimed at encouraging youth to think about how achieving goals in life is easier without marijuana. The What's Next campaign reinforces the fact that the majority of Colorado high school students do not use marijuana. It also shares information about how using marijuana can affect a teen's life now and in the future. The campaign provides adults with information about how to have an open and honest conversation with children about marijuana use.

When designing the program, the health department conducted research with more than eight hundred young Coloradans. Researchers found that teens do not want to listen to preachy messages about drugs or sit through scare tactics about the dangers of marijuana. Instead, the most effective prevention messages are those that talk about how marijuana can impact goals that mean something to a teen, such as getting a driver's license or doing well on a test. The health department plans to roll out the campaign across several media platforms, including a website, social media sites, online videos, a BuzzFeed partnership, and various youth events. "With retail

A New Jersey police officer talks to elementary school students as part of the Drug Abuse Resistance Education (D.A.R.E.) program. Experts agree that early interventions such as this help prevent a child's marijuana use later in life.

marijuana legal for adults in Colorado, preventing youth use becomes even more important," says Dr. Larry Wolk, health department executive director and chief medical officer. "We hope to further the conversation between young Coloradans, and the adults they trust, about the laws and about how using marijuana today could have implications that follow those youth into their futures."[70]

Zero-Tolerance Policies

According to the National Association of School Psychologists, many schools have a zero-tolerance policy for drug and alcohol use. If students commit any drug offense, such as having marijuana on school grounds, they are suspended or expelled from school, regardless of any extenuating circumstances. School officials who support zero-tolerance policies believe that if teens

Targeting High-Risk Kids

Researchers from the University of Montreal and CHU Sainte-Justine Children's Hospital in Montreal, Canada, may have found an effective way to prevent, reduce, or delay marijuana use in high-risk youth. The researchers worked with more than one thousand high-risk British students in ninth grade in London, as well as their teachers. The students took a personality assessment that identified those who were sensitive to anxiety and negative thinking, as well as those who were impulsive or sensation seeking, since these traits have been linked to a greater risk of substance abuse.

Students attended two ninety-minute cognitive behavioral sessions, customized to their personality type. The researchers then followed students over a two-year period. Overall, they found that high-risk students who participated in the program reduced marijuana use by 33 percent within the first six months after the sessions. The group of students at the greatest risk of marijuana use—the sensation seekers—experienced a 75 percent reduction in marijuana use six months after the intervention and significant reduction in use thereafter.

Quoted in University of Montreal, "Cannabis Use Can Be Prevented, Reduced or Delayed," ScienceDaily, May 26, 2015. www.sciencedaily.com.

know they will receive a specific and harsh punishment for marijuana use, it will deter them from using the drug.

Although many people believe that zero-tolerance policies deter marijuana use, studies have found that many such policies are ineffective. For example, a study published in the *American Journal of Public Health* in 2015 found that students who attend schools with suspension policies for illicit drug use were 1.6 times more likely than peers at schools without similar policies to use marijuana the next year. In the study, researchers reviewed samples of seventh- and ninth-grade students from Washington State and Victoria, Australia. Although demographically similar, schools in the two areas have very different approaches to drug use. In Victoria, schools focus on harm-minimization policies. When students are caught with marijuana, they are referred to a nurse or counselor or required to attend a drug cessation program. In contrast, Washington schools tend to have zero-tolerance policies with frequently enforced harsh punishments, such as expulsion or calling law enforcement. When comparing drug infractions at the two schools, Washington students were significantly more likely to be suspended if caught with drugs and about 50 percent more likely to be expelled.

When researchers looked at the effects of the zero-tolerance drug policies on student drug use, they found that most did not appear to significantly reduce marijuana use. In addition, mandatory suspensions actually increased the odds of drug use by 60 percent, even among students who had not been suspended. "That was surprising to us," says study coauthor Richard Catalano. "It means that suspensions are certainly not having a deterrent effect. It's just the opposite."[71] Calalano says that he believes that zero-tolerance policies that include suspensions can lead students to become disengaged from school, which encourages antisocial and delinquent behavior, smoking, and drug and alcohol use.

> "If we (suspend) these kids and they don't have a parental support system at home, we're just giving them a license to go and use more."[72]
>
> —Anthony Smith, principal of Adams City High School.

School-Based Treatment Programs

Recognizing that intervention rather than zero-tolerance may be more effective at preventing long-term marijuana use, a few schools offer treatment to students who are caught using marijuana at school. One such school, Adams City High School in Commerce City, Colorado, piloted a treatment program called Encompass in 2014. Instead of being punished, students caught using or under the influence of marijuana at school are allowed to enroll in the program. "It's a layered approach to discipline and treatment," says Anthony Smith, principal of Adams City High School. "If we (suspend) these kids and they don't have a parental support system at home, we're just giving them a license to go and use more."[72]

The Encompass program is an eight-week program that uses CBT to treat students. Students voluntarily enroll and then undergo a comprehensive psychiatric evaluation. According to Paula Riggs, director of the University of Colorado's division of substance dependence, most kids who have substance abuse problems also have at least one mental disorder such as depression or attention-deficit/hyperactivity disorder. "Almost every single one of these students is dependent on cannabis as a coping mechanism,"[73] says Riggs.

Over the course of the program, students meet with a therapist for nine hour-long sessions. At each session, the students take a urine drug test and then discuss triggers they faced that week. Each time a student attends a session, he or she gets to choose a reward chip from a fishbowl, which can be redeemed for prizes as simple as a compliment to up to one hundred dollars in vouchers. Students can earn more chips for each clean drug test and for positive activities like volunteering or sports. Riggs says that the chips create incentives for students to demonstrate healthy habits and live drug free. Although the program is in its infancy, the results appear promising. "Based on preliminary outcomes, we're getting significant reduction in substance abuse and many are achieving abstinence early on,"[74] Riggs says.

Early Intervention Key to Prevention

There are many factors that influence marijuana use, but experts agree that early intervention is the key to successfully preventing marijuana abuse or reducing its harmful effects. As more states legalize marijuana for medical and recreational use, more young people believe that marijuana is not harmful. "We're seeing that there's a great increase in youth marijuana usage as the perception of harm has really fallen off," says Devin Bradley, Nevada County public health education specialist. "Young people don't think it's harmful. They don't think it's dangerous."[75] Yet research has shown that marijuana is harmful to the adolescent brain. Therefore, prevention efforts that target kids at young ages, before they experiment with marijuana for the first time, and teach them the real risks and dangers of marijuana are an important part of reducing marijuana use and abuse.

SOURCE NOTES

Chapter 1: The Scope of Marijuana Use

1. Quoted in Michael Goot, "A Dose of Reality: South High Panel Talks About Prevalence of Pot Use Among Students," *Glens Falls (NY) Post-Star*, October 30, 2014. http://poststar.com.
2. Quoted in Goot, "A Dose of Reality."
3. Quoted in Brigid Shulte, "Even Where It's Legal for Parents to Smoke Pot: What About the Kids?," *Washington Post*, June 6, 2015. www.washingtonpost.com.
4. Quoted in Christine Rushton, "Teens Find a New Use for E-cigarettes: Vaping Marijuana," *USA Today*, September 7, 2015. www.usatoday.com.
5. Quoted in Miles Bryan, "Pot Smoke and Mirrors: Vaporizer Pens Hide Marijuana Use," *Morning Edition*, NPR, April 18, 2014. www.npr.org.
6. Quoted in Bryan, "Pot Smoke and Mirrors."
7. Quoted in Jessie Wardarski, "Edible Marijuana Is Booming, but These Aren't Your Father's Pot Brownies," NBC News, August 19, 2015. www.nbcnews.com.
8. Quoted in Deb Stanley and Jennifer Kovaleski, "CDC Issues Report on Marijuana Cookie Death; Student Levy Thamba Pongi Jumped from Balcony," Denver Channel, July 24, 2015. www.thedenverchannel.com.
9. Jessica B. Hancock-Allen et al., "Notes from the Field: Death Following Ingestion of an Edible Marijuana Product—Colorado, March 2014," *Morbidity and Mortality Weekly Report*, July 24, 2015. www.cdc.gov.
10. Quoted in Anthony Rivas, "Dabs, a Marijuana Concentrate, Is Becoming More Popular: But Is It Dangerous?," Medical Daily, June 15, 2015. www.medicaldaily.com.
11. Quoted in Katie Huinker, "Special Report: Marijuana Concentrates Grow in Popularity," KIMT 3, April 27, 2015. http://kimt.com.
12. Quoted in Rivas, "Dabs, a Marijuana Concentrate, Is Becoming More Popular."

13. Quoted in Robert McCoppin and Dan Moran, "Medical Marijuana Debuts in Illinois but Some Patients Turned Away," *Chicago Tribune*, November 9, 2015. www.chicagotribune.com.
14. Quoted in Sarah Williams, "National Survey Shows Fewer Teens See Marijuana Use as Risky," *MinnPost*, December 18, 2013. www.minnpost.com.
15. Quoted in Trevor Hughes, "Poll Says Marijuana Legalization Support Nears 60%," *USA Today*, October 21, 2015. www.usatoday.com.

Chapter 2: Effects of Marijuana Use

16. Quoted in Physician Health Services, "Success Story: Reasons to Give—a Personal Story," 2016. www.massmed.org.
17. Quoted in R. Douglas Fields, "Creativity, Madness, and Drugs," *MIND Guest Blog*, *Scientific American*, November 22, 2013. http://blogs.scientificamerican.com.
18. Quoted in Sonny Sea Gold, "Stoned Age: The Real Risks of Getting High," *Teen Vogue*, November 4, 2014. www.teenvogue.com.
19. Quoted in Gold, "Stoned Age."
20. Maureen Dowd, "Don't Harsh Our Mellow, Dude," *New York Times*, June 3, 2014. www.nytimes.com.
21. Quoted in Rene Marsh, "Fed Study: Booze Impact Greater than Pot on Driving," CNN, June 25, 2015. www.cnn.com.
22. Quoted in CBS Seattle, "Study: Fatal Car Crashes Involving Marijuana Have Tripled," February 4, 2014. http://seattle.cbslocal.com.
23. Quoted in Patti Neighmond, "Marijuana May Hurt the Developing Teen Brain," *Morning Edition*, NPR, March 3, 2014. www.npr.org.
24. Quoted in Maia Szalavitz, "Does Marijuana Use by Teens Really Cause a Drop in IQ?," *Time*, August 28, 2012. http://healthland.time.com.
25. Quoted in Neighmond, "Marijuana May Hurt the Developing Teen Brain."
26. Quoted in Saundra Young, "Frequent Teen Marijuana Use Linked to Issues Later in Life," CNN, September 10, 2014. www.cnn.com.
27. National Alliance on Mental Illness, "Marijuana and Mental Illness," 2013. www2.nami.org.
28. Quoted in Sergio Prostak, "Study Confirms AKT1 Genotype Contributes to Risk of Cannabis Psychosis," Sci-News.com, November 15, 2012. www.sci-news.com.

29. Quoted in American Psychological Association, "Teen Marijuana Use Not Linked to Later Depression, Lung Cancer, Other Health Problems, Research Finds," August 4, 2015. www.apa.org.
30. Quoted in Hampton Sides, "High Science," *National Geographic*, June 2015, p. 55.

Chapter 3: How Addictive Is Marijuana?

31. Quoted in Rachel Barclay, "Marijuana Addiction Is Rare, but Very Real," Healthline, June 20, 2014. www.healthline.com.
32. Quoted in Gold, "Stoned Age."
33. Quoted in Marianne McCune, "From Marijuana to the Medicine Cabinet: A Boy Who Couldn't Stop," WNYC News, May 10, 2013. www.wnyc.org.
34. Quoted in McCune, "From Marijuana to the Medicine Cabinet."
35. Quoted in Barclay, "Marijuana Addiction Is Rare, but Very Real."
36. Quoted in Barclay, "Marijuana Addiction Is Rare, but Very Real."
37. Quoted in Barclay, "Marijuana Addiction Is Rare, but Very Real."
38. Quoted in Cathy Payne and Michelle Healy, "Marijuana's Health Effects: Memory Problems, Addiction," *USA Today*, December 7, 2012. www.usatoday.com.
39. Quoted in Barclay, "Marijuana Addiction Is Rare, but Very Real."
40. Quoted in McCune, "From Marijuana to the Medicine Cabinet."
41. Quoted in McCune, "From Marijuana to the Medicine Cabinet."
42. Quoted in Barclay, "Marijuana Addiction Is Rare, but Very Real."
43. Quoted in Barclay, "Marijuana Addiction Is Rare, but Very Real."
44. Quoted in Molly Oswaks, "What Smoking Weed Can Do to Your Relationship," *Cosmopolitan*, August 8, 2015. www.cosmopolitan.com.
45. Quoted in McCune, "From Marijuana to the Medicine Cabinet."
46. Quoted in Prevent Teen Drug Use, "A Teen's Story," November 16, 2011. www.preventteendruguse.org.
47. Quoted in Gerry Everding, "Marijuana Dependence Influenced by Genes, Childhood Sexual Abuse," Washington University in St. Louis, November 16, 2015. http://news.wustl.edu.
48. Quoted in Everding, "Marijuana Dependence Influenced by Genes, Childhood Sexual Abuse."
49. Quoted in Barclay, "Marijuana Addiction Is Rare, but Very Real."
50. Quoted in Barclay, "Marijuana Addiction Is Rare, but Very Real."
51. Quoted in Hughes, "Poll Says Marijuana Legalization Support Nears 60%."

Chapter 4: Challenges of Treatment and Recovery

52. Quoted in Jenny Brundin, "Addicted Teen Struggles to Break Marijuana Habit," Colorado Public Radio, March 20, 2014. www.cpr.org.

53. Quoted in Brundin, "Addicted Teen Struggles to Break Marijuana Habit."

54. Quoted in Brundin, "Addicted Teen Struggles to Break Marijuana Habit."

55. Lynn O'Connor, "Marijuana Addiction Today: Marijuana Addiction Is Real, Widespread, and Treatable," *Our Empathic Nature* (blog), *Psychology Today*, May 2, 2012. www.psychologytoday.com.

56. Quoted in Kathleen Richards, "Is Marijuana Addictive? A Look at the Scientific Research," *Seattle Stranger*, April 13, 2015. www.thestranger.com.

57. Quoted in Kelly Riddell, "Marijuana Addiction Drug Research Gets $3 Million Grant as Obama Encourages Legalization," *Washington Times*, June 25, 2015. www.washingtontimes.com.

58. Quoted in Claire Martin, "No Joke: About 9 Percent of Marijuana Users Risk Addiction," *Denver Post*, December 26, 2014. www.denverpost.com.

59. Quoted in Janice Wood, "Some Withdrawal Symptoms Linked to Relapse for Marijuana Users," Psych Central, September 27, 2012. http://psychcentral.com.

60. O'Connor, "Marijuana Addiction Today."

61. Physician's Health Services, "Success Story: Reasons to Give, a Personal Story," Physicians Health Services. www.massmed.org.

62. Physicians Health Services, "Success Story."

Chapter 5: Preventing Marijuana Use

63. Quoted in North Carolina State University, "Parents Key to Preventing Alcohol, Marijuana Use by Kids," ScienceDaily, December 4, 2012. www.sciencedaily.com.

64. Quoted in Kathy Samudovsky, "Strengthening Families Program Aims to Help Middle Schoolers and Their Parents," *Pittsburgh Post-Gazette*, January 22, 2015. www.post-gazette.com.

65. Quoted in Samudovsky, "Strengthening Families Program Aims to Help Middle Schoolers and Their Parents."

66. Quoted in City of Boston, "Mayor Walsh Joins Boston Public Schools in Announcing Partnership with the Gavin Foundation and UMass Boston," March 3, 2015. www.cityofboston.gov.

67. Quoted in Alexandra Pannoni, "3 Ways High Schools Are Combating Marijuana Use," *U.S. News & World Report*, September 15, 2014. www.usnews.com.

68. Quoted in Katie Levingston, "In Boston, Preventing Substance Abuse Starts in Middle School," Boston.com, March 5, 2015. www.boston.com.

69. Quoted in Levingston, "In Boston, Preventing Substance Abuse Starts in Middle School."

70. Quoted in David Brendsel, "State Health Department Launches Youth Marijuana Education and Prevention Campaign," Colorado Department of Public Health & Environment, August 19, 2015. www.colorado.gov.

71. Quoted in Christopher Ingraham, "Zero-Tolerance School Drug Policies Only Make Drug Use Worse, a Study Finds," *Washington Post*, March 23, 2015. www.washingtonpost.com.

72. Quoted in Megan Mitchell, "Adams City High in Commerce City Offers Pot Offenders Treatment Option," *Denver Post*, April 10, 2014. www.denverpost.com.

73. Quoted in Mitchell, "Adams City High in Commerce City Offers Pot Offenders Treatment Option."

74. Quoted in Mitchell, "Adams City High in Commerce City Offers Pot Offenders Treatment Option."

75. Quoted in Margaret Moran, "Curbing Tahoe-Truckee Youth Pot Use Key to Stopping Abuse, Officials Say," *Sierra Sun* (Truckee and Tahoe City, CA), September 16, 2015. www.sierrasun.com.

ORGANIZATIONS TO CONTACT

Community Anti-Drug Coalitions of America (CADCA)
625 Slaters Ln., Suite 300
Alexandria, VA 22314
phone: (800) 542-2322 • fax: (703) 706-0565
e-mail: info@cadca.org • website: www.cadca.org

Representing more than five thousand community coalitions and affiliates, the CADCA seeks to make America's communities safe, healthy, and drug free. Its website offers policy information, news articles, and other information about many drugs, including marijuana.

Drug Free America Foundation
5999 Central Ave., Suite 301
Saint Petersburg, FL 33710
phone: (727) 828-0211 • fax: (727) 828-0212
e-mail: webmaster@dfaf.org • website: www.dfaf.org

The Drug Free America Foundation is a drug-prevention and drug policy organization. Its website has news and articles about many drugs and prevention initiatives, including those focused on marijuana.

Drug Policy Alliance
131 W. Thirty-Third St., 15th Floor
New York, NY 10001
phone: (212) 613-8020 • fax: (212) 613-8021
e-mail: nyc@drugpolicy.org • website: www.drugpolicy.org

The Drug Policy Alliance promotes alternatives to current drug policy that are grounded in science, compassion, health, and human rights. Its website features drug facts, statistics, information about drug laws, and articles about numerous drugs, including marijuana.

Foundation for a Drug-Free World
1626 N. Wilcox Ave., Suite 1297
Los Angeles, CA 90028
phone: (818) 952-5260 • toll-free: (888) 668-6378
e-mail: info@drugfreeworld.org • website: www.drugfreeworld.org

The Foundation for a Drug-Free World provides factual information about drugs to youth and adults to help them make informed decisions and live drug free. A wealth of information is available on the interactive website, including articles specifically related to marijuana abuse.

Marijuana Anonymous (MA)

Marijuana Anonymous World Services
340 S. Lemon Ave., #9420
Walnut, CA 91789-2706
phone: (800) 766-6779
e-mail: office@marijuana-anonymous.org
website: www.marijuana-anonymous.org

MA is a support group for people working to recover from marijuana addiction. MA uses the 12 Steps of Recovery founded by Alcoholics Anonymous. Its website features information on addiction and recovery, as well as personal stories about marijuana addiction.

Marijuana Policy Project (MPP)

PO Box 77492
Capitol Hill Station
Washington, DC 20013
phone: (202) 462-5747
e-mail: info@mpp.org • website: www.mpp.org

Founded in 1995, the MPP is the largest organization in the United States that focuses on ending marijuana prohibition. The MPP works to change federal law to allow states to determine their own marijuana policies and has been an integral part of changing state marijuana laws, including those in Colorado and Alaska.

National Institute on Drug Abuse (NIDA)

National Institutes of Health
6001 Executive Blvd., Room 5213
Bethesda, MD 20892-9561
phone: (301) 443-1124
e-mail: information@nida.nih.gov • website: www.drugabuse.gov

The NIDA supports research efforts that improve drug-abuse prevention, treatment, and policy. The website links to a separate NIDA for Teens site, which is designed especially for young people and provides a wealth of information about drugs, including marijuana.

Office of National Drug Control Policy (ONDCP)

750 Seventeenth St. NW
Washington, DC 20503
phone: (800) 666-3332 • fax: (202) 395-6708
e-mail: ondcp@ncjrs.org • website: www.whitehouse.gov/ondcp

A component of the Executive Office of the President, the ONDCP is responsible for directing the federal government's antidrug programs. A wide variety of publications about marijuana can be found on the site.

Partnership for Drug-Free Kids

352 Park Ave. S., 9th Floor
New York, NY 10010
phone: (212) 922-1560 • fax: (212) 922-1570
website: www.drugfree.org

The Partnership for Drug-Free Kids is dedicated to helping parents and families solve the problem of teenage substance abuse. A large number of informative publications and current articles about marijuana are available on its website.

Substance Abuse and Mental Health Services Administration (SAMHSA)

1 Choke Cherry Rd.
Rockville, MD 20857
phone: (877) 726-4727 • fax: (240) 221-4292
e-mail: samhsainfo@samhsa.hhs.gov • website: www.samhsa.gov

SAMHSA's mission is to reduce the impact of substance abuse and mental illness on America's communities. The site offers numerous articles, fact sheets, and other types of publications about marijuana.

US Drug Enforcement Administration (DEA)

8701 Morrissette Dr.
Springfield, VA 22152
phone: (202) 307-1000
website: www.dea.gov • teen website: www.justthinktwice.com

An agency of the US Department of Justice, the DEA is the United States' leading law enforcement agency for combating the sale and distribution of narcotics and other illegal drugs. Its website links to a separate teen site that provides a wealth of information about drugs, including marijuana.

FOR FURTHER RESEARCH

Books

John Allen, *Thinking Critically: Legalizing Marijuana*. San Diego, CA: ReferencePoint, 2015.

Daniel Benjamin, *Marijuana*. New York: Cavendish Square, 2012.

Noah Berlatsky, *Marijuana*. Farmington Hills, MI: Greenhaven, 2012.

Leanne Currie-McGhee, *Teens and Marijuana*. San Diego, CA: ReferencePoint, 2015.

Arthur Gillard, *Medical Marijuana*. Farmington Hills, MI: Greenhaven, 2013.

Patricia D. Netzley, *Is Legalized Marijuana Good for Society?* San Diego, CA: ReferencePoint, 2015.

E.J. Sanna, *Marijuana: Mind-Altering Weed*. Broomall, PA: Mason Crest, 2012.

Internet Sources

Drug Enforcement Administration, "The Dangers and Consequences of Marijuana Abuse," 2014. www.dea.gov/docs/dangers-consequences -marijuana-abuse.pdf.

Drug Enforcement Administration, "Drug Fact Sheet: Marijuana." www .dea.gov/druginfo/drug_data_sheets/Marijuana.pdf.

National Alliance on Mental Illness, "Marijuana and Mental Illness," 2013. www2.nami.org/factsheets/marijuana_factsheet.pdf.

National Institute on Drug Abuse, "Marijuana: Facts for Teens," 2015. www.drugabuse.gov/publications/marijuana-facts-teens/letter-to -teens.

Patti Neighmond, "Marijuana May Hurt the Developing Teen Brain," *Morning Edition*, NPR, March 3, 2014. www.npr.org/sections/health -shots/2014/02/25/282631913/marijuana-may-hurt-the-developing -teen-brain.

Office of National Drug Control Policy, "Marijuana: Know the Facts," 2012. www.whitehouse.gov/sites/default/files/page/files/marijuana_fact _sheet_3-28-12.pdf.

Cathy Payne and Michelle Healy, "Marijuana's Health Effects: Memory Problems, Addiction," *USA Today*, December 7, 2012. www.usatoday .com/story/news/nation/2012/12/06/nih-marijuana-effects/1751011.

Substance Abuse and Mental Health Services Administration, "Behavioral Health Trends in the United States: Results from the 2014 National Survey on Drug Use and Health," 2015. www.samhsa.gov/data/sites /default/files/NSDUH-FRR1-2014/NSDUH-FRR1-2014.pdf.

Jessie Wardarski, "Edible Marijuana Is Booming, but These Aren't Your Father's Pot Brownies," NBC News, August 19, 2015. www.nbcnews .com/health/health-news/these-are-not-your-fathers-pot-brownies -n411881.

Websites

Just Think Twice (www.justthinktwice.com). An antidrug website that give teens information, news, true stories, consequences, and facts about drugs and addiction, including marijuana.

Learn About Marijuana (http://learnaboutmarijuanawa.org). This website is sponsored by multiple Washington state agencies, including the Alcohol and Drug Abuse Institute at the University of Washington, to provide marijuana information to the public.

Marijuana in Colorado (www.colorado.gov/marijuana). This website from the state of Colorado provides information about the legalization of marijuana in Colorado and the health effects and responsible use of retail marijuana.

What's with Weed (www.whatswithweed.ca). This website is geared toward marijuana users, friends of users, and those thinking about using. It provides information about how marijuana affects different people and how to avoid negative outcomes.

INDEX

PICTURE CREDITS